Path of Light
A Masonic Journey

by Michael R. Poll

A Cornerstone Book

Path of Light
A Masonic Journey
by Michael R. Poll

A Cornerstone Book
Published by Cornerstone Book Publishers

Cornerstone Book Publishers
Hot Springs Village, AR
www.cornerstonepublishers.com

First Cornerstone Edition – 2023

ISBN: 978-1613426999

Table of Contents

Introduction

I'm looking out my window on the first day of a brand-new year. I see small birds flying to the ground and pecking for something in the leaves. Just a few moments ago, squirrels were searching through the very same spots. I saw one pick up an acorn, sit on his back legs, and quickly grab a few bits of it while holding it in his tiny hands. For some reason, all the squirrels then scattered and were replaced by other birds. All of them were searching in a rush and seemed to have little time to spare.

Everything I see out of my window is done from the warmth of my home. I'm sitting at my desk in a comfortable chair. I have good food available only steps away in my kitchen. I have my family near me, a comfortable bed, nice clothes, books, all sorts of electronic entertainment, and a sturdy roof over my head. I must be much more important than these pitiful creatures outside my window. They have nothing and don't even know if they will be alive later today. But, then again, is my being alive later today something of which I am so certain? What do I (we) *really* have that makes us so much more important than other forms of life? What is the difference between our lifeless bodies and their lifeless bodies?

Some might say that knowledge of the Almighty separates us from the animal kingdom, but I am not so sure. It might well be ego. How do I know what a small bird knows? I only assume it is mindless because I can't communicate with it. I know that scientists have analyzed its brain, but what does that tell me about if or how they may be able to think, feel, or know? I don't really know how I am able to think. There is so very much without answers.

My decision is that I will respect and admire all life. I will do all in my power to grow in mind and spirit. I will try never to be in the way of the growth of any being. I desire only harmony in life. That's the path I choose to travel.

This book is a journal of discovery, thoughts, and questions. I admit that I wrote this book for myself. It is a lifelong quest for any dedicated Mason to understand our Masonic philosophy. The truth is that the thoughts and ideas offered here are for my benefit to help me find my path in the darkness. If what is offered in this or any of my works benefits you, then I am happy. My sole goal is to seek light; if I can help others in the darkness, I am rewarded.

Peace.

Michael R. Poll
January 1, 2023

Path of Light

Blind Truth and Justice

Specific words and how they are understood play a considerable role in Masonic allegories as well as daily life. How particular words are used or arranged can affect how something is understood or misunderstood. Justice and truth are core words that can be understood with more than one meaning. They are also words that can be a source of misunderstanding. For example, if we add the word "blind" to either of them, it can change the meaning. An explanation becomes necessary to understand what we mean. Let's look at this situation and a few examples.

Truth is something that is not false. Truth is proven to be so and is a factual state of reality. But if we say that someone is blind to the truth, that means they do not recognize the truth when it is provided. If someone writes that Frank Smith was made a Mason on a certain date and then supports the statement with records from his lodge and Grand Lodge, it is reasonable to say that Frank Smith *was* made a Mason on the date stated. We can accept it as fact. For someone to be unable to accept the records of the lodge and Grand Lodge could be described as "blind to the truth." When presented with the truth, they could not *see* it or, maybe, understand it.

The term "Blind Justice" is often depicted by a blindfolded "Lady Justice." This statute suggests that justice should be impartially rendered with no pre-judgment (positive or negative) of whatever or whoever is under examination. It should be fair for all and equally administered to and for everyone's benefit. This concept of fair justice goes back to the 1500s but was not always understood as it is today. In fact, it was initially understood to mean exactly the opposite of what it means today. Originally the blindfolded "Lady Justice" was a plea for help and a sarcastic symbolic statement that justice could be "blind" to the truth. Justice for the poor was different from justice for the wealthy. Symbols and their meanings can change.

There is another type of truth that, if coupled with justice, can create trust issues with any leadership. It is often identified as an "inconvenient truth." This is a type of truth that is not accepted or acknowledged even if proven to be fact. This truth is rejected because it is disliked or felt to be problematic for an already accepted, desirable idea. It is inconvenient because if accepted, it would require changes that are not wanted. If an individual holds such an opinion, they can be said to be foolish. But it is the right of all individuals to believe however they choose. But such an opinion held by any organized leadership creates reasonable trust issues that can permanently damage the group's reputation. In other words, individuals can believe whatever they wish, even nonsense. This is because they affect only themselves. Yes, it will hurt their reputation and give others cause to discount them and their opinions, but that is the right of every individual. But one who takes on any leadership office or position of influence with any type of organization is responsible for more than just their own reputation.

When we join the leadership of any organization, we are responsible for more than our personal reputation. How others view us will be how they view the organization. If we have a history of being knowingly "blind to the truth" or reject what is proven, then we will *not* be viewed as being able to dispense justice or fairly evaluate any question impartially. We will be viewed as having ulterior motives in what we say and do. We will not be trusted because when facts are presented, we might refuse to acknowledge them in favor of personal desires.

In addition to the above, any honest, sincere person can make a mistake. We may believe something is true, only to discover that we have been mistaken. We may also care deeply about an organization, so deeply that we may make the error of knowingly allowing an untruth to be accepted as the truth. We may believe that a falsehood is better for an organization than the truth. It is in these situations where our integrity is tested.

But what about when "truth" is not provable, and all that is available are opinions and beliefs? We can't label the unproven as either truth or falsehood. Justice demands that we remain open and objective. If fact cannot be determined, we must clearly identify anything we write or say as an opinion. It is OK to have a clear opinion about a situation or aspect of history that is unproven. Still, we must be ready to change even firmly held opinions if facts are discovered. We must not write or say something is a fact if it is not proven or provable. We must never hide or cover up facts that disprove our opinion.

And this all brings us back to words and how we use them. What we think, believe, or can prove is only of value if we can properly convey those thoughts in spoken and written words. As far as understanding, the spoken word often has an advantage over things we write. The advantage is that what we speak often has body language and inflections in our voice to assist with subtle meanings. The written word is naked communication. How we are understood depends on what we write and the words we choose to express our thoughts and ideas. Our opportunities for misunderstanding are far greater with the written word than with speech.

When we attempt to present either opinions or facts with the written word, care must be taken so that we are clear in what we are writing. Too often, college term papers come to mind when the inexperienced writer attempts to offer an idea. We have concerns that what we write will be judged for its academic value. We may look at our paper and think that *this* and *this* are a far more impressive words that will show others our command of language. We must always remember that we should write to communicate, not impress. The best forms of communication are ideas expressed in simple terms. We often miss the mark if we write to show off our language skills. A clear, sound idea can be confused if our word selection is guided by attempts to *find the biggest word* rather than educate. A paper with perfect grammar can utterly fail to communicate a desired thought or fact.

Rhetoric is one of the seven Liberal Arts and Sciences that we learn about in Masonry, but it is often mistaken for the "memorization of our rituals." Rhetoric is the proper use of language to communicate and teach. Our goal as Freemasons is to learn and then pass on what we have learned. Our lessons of integrity teach us to seek and accept only the truth. Justice must guide our hands and thoughts. We do not serve Freemasonry or any organization of Freemasonry with half-truths or unclear, misleading truths. If the truth is inconvenient, it is still the truth. Our integrity will determine if we advance the truth or hide it in misleading words or smoke. Justice will either be served or denied by our words and actions. Write well.

Masonic Rites, Appendant Bodies, and Confusion

I remember when I first joined Freemasonry. An old Past Master pulled me aside and told me, "You are joining a true college. A great college! You can find more valuable education in Masonry than you can imagine." After over 45 years of being a Mason, I very much agree with that old Past Master. I believe that I will continue to learn from Masonry until my last day. It is a seemingly bottomless well of available, valuable wisdom. But the burden is on me to do the work of study.

In 1875, Albert Mackey wrote a paper titled *"Reading Masons and Masons Who Do Not Read."* In that paper, he ended it with a most interesting line, "The ultimate success of Masonry depends on the intelligence of her disciples."[1] I find that a fascinating statement as he seems to qualify the "ultimate success" of Freemasonry as well as the intelligence of its members. Mackey is not telling us that Masonry is successful because of the intelligence of its members. He is telling us that Masonry *will be* successful *if* it has intelligent, reading members. Our lodges will have intelligent members if the lodges provide quality Masonic education and if our members take advantage of the education offered. If the lodges provide nothing more than a hot meal and a reading of the minutes, or if the members turn their back on Masonic education when it is offered, then the "ultimate success" that Brother Mackey spoke of will not occur.

The level of success that a lodge enjoys often depends on the level of comprehension and mastery of a wide array of Masonic educational subjects available to the members. For example, a successful lodge does not require every member to be proficient in the ritual. But its officers and a significant portion of the lodge will undoubtedly have such ability in successful lodges. We must understand certain basics for the lodge's success and personal growth.

An often glossed-over yet significant aspect of Masonic education is the nature of Masonic Rites. It seems that many in the US today confuse or have but limited understanding of the differences between a Masonic Rite and an appendant body. In fact, some have very firmly held incorrect opinions. A Masonic Rite and an appendant body are different things and understanding them is very much a part of a solid plan of Masonic education.

In the US, it is common today to believe that an appendant body is pretty much anything other than a craft lodge. Too often, I read in US Masonic publications and hear in lectures that the York Rite and the Scottish Rite are *appendant bodies*. Such a belief differs from the original understanding of how Rites were viewed and is different from how they are currently recognized in most areas outside the United States. Regardless, today the York Rite and Scottish Rite are often listed alongside organizations such as the Shriners, Grotto, Eastern Star, etc. When questioned why these two Rites are considered appendant, I'm usually either given a blank stare or told the bodies are "appendant" or "attached to" the craft lodge. I'm told they are organizations a Mason can join after receiving his Master Mason degree. That's a misunderstanding of the nature of a Masonic Rite. Of course, groups such as the Shriners, the Grotto, the Eastern Star, and others *are* appendant bodies. As a prerequisite, many of these organizations require membership in a craft lodge (obtaining the Master Mason degree). And here seems to be the source of a long-held confusion about Masonic Rites.

So, why would I say that the York and Scottish Rites differ from the Shrine, Grotto, etc.? Why do I say that they are *not* appendant bodies? Well, as their names suggest, the York Rite and the Scottish Rite are Masonic *Rites* or systems of Freemasonry. A Rite, or system of Freemasonry, is a collection of unique rituals beginning in the entered apprentice degree and concluding in whatever is their final degree. As Albert Mackey tells us:

"The original system of Speculative Masonry consisted only of the three Symbolic degrees called, therefore, Ancient Craft Masonry. Such was the condition of Freemasonry at the time of what is called the revival of 1717. Hence, this was the original Rite or approved usage, and so it continued in England until the year 1813, when at the union of the two Grand Lodges, the "Holy Royal Arch" was declared to be part of the system; and thus, the English Rite was made legitimately to consist of four degrees.
But on the Continent of Europe, the organization of new systems began at a much earlier period, and by the invention of what are known as

the high degrees a multitude of Rites were established. All of these agreed in one important essential. They were built upon the three Symbolic degrees which in every instance constituted the fundamental basis upon which they were erected."[2]

The important point is that while a Masonic Rite is a collection of rituals that are similar or related in content, it is not an organization itself. A Masonic Rite is not under the jurisdiction of any Masonic body or organization. A Masonic body uses or works in the rituals of a Masonic Rite.

A Masonic ritual is the script used to confer degrees, open lodges, and is the words of our catechism. A regular Masonic craft ritual will contain the Hiramic Legend. And while the three craft degrees follow a logical storyline, they can sometimes be quite different from other rituals of the same degree. These differences can be looked at as the various *Rites* of Freemasonry. The Scottish Rite and the York Rite are both considered *Rites* because they start with their own unique craft lodge degrees and rituals. You can think of the different Rites as different ways of telling the same story.

Over time, translators and editors changed rituals depending on the lodges using the rituals or what was felt to be important for Masons in particular areas. For instance, a language problem existed when Speculative Freemasonry was taken from England to France in its early days. It was necessary to translate the English craft rituals into French if there was any hope of successfully spreading Freemasonry in France. When this translation was done, some consideration for French culture was given. The French rituals told the same story as the English rituals, but how the story was told became a bit different in the French versions; this evolved into the French Rite.

When we compare early English and French rituals, it is easy to see that the French rituals became more theatrical. The French rituals also spent more time on aspects of symbolism than the English. This has much to do with the two cultures, and the differences in the rituals reflect the differences between those two cultures. But what does it mean in practice to have different rituals? In the New Orleans area, you can today see two forms of Masonic craft rituals (two Rites) in practice,[3] and both in the English language. One is the York Rite craft ritual (English in nature), and the other is the Scottish Rite craft ritual (French in nature). In a nutshell, the York Rite craft ritual is the foundation of the rest of the degrees of the system known in the US as the York Rite.[4] The Scottish Rite craft ritual is the foundation of the degrees of the Scottish Rite from the 4th to the 33rd (the rest of that system). In many places outside the US, you can see two or more different craft rituals (different Rites) being worked.

Because the evolution of the Masonic Rites seemed to be a bit haphazard (with new Rites and rituals springing up almost at will), they can vary in the number of degrees and even the subject matter of the degrees above the third. A Mason completing the degrees of one Rite will receive a different Masonic experience than a Mason of another Rite. Yes, there is a relationship between the various Rites, but also clear differences. Masonic bodies working in the various Rites today can be seen as selectively exclusive in membership.

(9)

LIST OF LODGES IN ACTIVITY

UNDER THE JURISDICTION OF THE GRAND LODGE OF THE STATE OF LOUISIANA.

LODGES OF YORK RITE,

Meeting at New Orleans, in Rampart street.

No 1. PERFECT UNION—Founder of the Grand Lodge.—Lucien Hermann, Master ; H. B. Cenas, S. W. ; Louis Le-beau, J. W.

At New Orleans, in Urselines street.

No. 3. CONCORD—Founder of the Grand Lodge.—J. M. Moreau, Master ; F. L. Reinecke, S. W. ; P. A. Huard, J. W.

At New Orleans in St. Claude street.

No. 4. PERSEVERANCE—Founder of the Grand Lodge.—Francis Calongne, Master ; Jules Durrive, S. W. ; Thomas Bell, J. W.

At St. Landry, Opelousas.

No. 19. THE HUMBLE COTTAGE.—C. H. Lewis, Master ; Evariste Debaillon, S. W. ; B. K. Rogers, J. W.

At St. Francisville, West Feliciana.

No. 31. FELICIANA.—Eugene Remondet, Master ; W. B. Clupton, S. W. ; J. M. Baker, J. W.

At Alexandria, Louisiana.

No. 37. ALEXANDRIA.—William B. Hyman, Master ; Allen Tuck, S. W. ; Jackson Farrar, J. W.

At Natchitoches, Louisiana.

No. 38. PHENIX.—P. A. Morse, Master ; F. Williams, S. W. ; N. ———, J. W.

At New Orleans, corner of Common and Tchoupitoulas streets.

No. 39. POINSETT.—A. S. Douglass, Master ; H. M. Summers, S. W. ; W. H. Van Reuselear, J. W.

At Napoleonville, Parish of Assumption.

No. 44. DESERT.—Clodius Linosier, Master ; J. A. Guerard, S. W. ; Charles Monot, J. W.

At Greenwood, Parish of Caddo.

No 45. JACKSON.—Alfred Flournoy, Master ; D. J. Hooks, S. W. ; A. G. Tuqua, J. W.

2

(10)

At New Orleans, at Perseverance Lodge.

No. 46. GERMANIA.—Gustavus Martel, Master ; Liebman Rose, S. W. ; Theobald Kœning, J. W.

At East Baton Rouge.

No. 47. ST. JAMES LODGE.—D. F. Reeder, Master ; J. L. Lobdell, S. W. ; P. Cain, J. W.

At St. Martinsville, Attakapas.

No. 48. L'HOSPITALIERE DU TECHE—Cornelius Voorhic, Master ; J. B. Derbes, S. W. ; V. A. Fournet, J. W.

At Shreveport, Parish of Caddo.

No. 49. CADDO.—Joel W. Hardwich, Master ; L. P. Crain, S. W. ; A. T. Alfred, J. W.

LODGES OF THE SCOTCH RITE,

Accumulating the York and Modern Rites.

At New Orleans, in Love street.

No. 1. POLAR STAR—Founder of the Grand Lodge.—Felix Garcia, Master ; R. Brugier, S. W. ; James Poupart, J. W.

At New Orleans in Plauché street.

No. 3. LIBERAL.—Adrian Nautré, Master ; Henry Train, S. W. ; Simon Viot, J. W.

At New Orleans, at Perfect Union Lodge.

No. 4. FRATERNAL LOVE.—J. M. Labarre, Master ; J. J. Rico, S. W. ; M. F. de la Vega, J. W.

At New Orleans, at Perseverance Lodge.

No. 5. THE FRIENDS OF THE ORDER.—Rafael Sagrera, Master ; John Bachino, S. W. ; Peter Casanas, J. W.

LODGES OF MODERN RITE,

Accumulating the Scotch and York Rites.

At New Orleans, in Plauché street.

No. 4. MASONIC HEARTH.—Antoine Mondelli, Master ; Joseph Barnes, S. W. ; E. Bertrand, J. W.

From the 1845 Proceedings of the Grand Lodge of Louisiana. Craft lodges were listed together according to their Masonic Rite.

A Master Mason cannot visit Masonic bodies or degrees he has not received. In addition, if one has received all the degrees available in one Rite, he is still not entitled to visit corresponding degrees in bodies of other Rites unless he holds membership there as well. But what about a Master Mason in a Scottish Rite craft lodge in New Orleans (or elsewhere)? Can he visit a York Rite lodge of Master Masons?[5] Mackey again instructs us:

> "Hence arises the law, that whatever may be the constitution and teachings of any Rite as to the higher degrees peculiar to it, the three Symbolic degrees being common to all the Rites, a Master Mason, in any one of the Rites, may visit and labor in a Master's Lodge of every other Rite. It is only after that degree is passed that the exclusiveness of each Rite begins to operate."[6]

Yes, a Master Mason in a Scottish Rite craft lodge may visit, and even join, a York Rite craft lodge in New Orleans or elsewhere (and vice-versa).[7] It is part of the education in New Orleans area craft lodges to witness the differences in the rituals of craft lodges available there and begin their understanding of Masonic Rites. It becomes clear to the New Orleans area Scottish Rite craft Masons that their ritual is the foundation of the whole Scottish Rite. Those Scottish Rite Craft Masons who go on to join a Scottish Rite valley in the Southern Jurisdiction will see that the "storyline" between their 3rd degree and the 4th degree in a valley is a natural progression of their Scottish Rite ritual. Members of a York Rite craft lodge find the 4th degree of the Scottish Rite as recognizable but not a natural flow in their ritual or storyline of the Hiramic Legend. It is clear to a York Rite craft Mason that they have walked into a different version of the ritual account in their craft lodge.

But, if the Scottish Rite craft rituals (and craft lodges) are the foundation of the Scottish Rite degrees from the 4th to the 33rd, why are these lodges so very rare in the United States? Let's look at it.

We can see some interesting developments in Freemasonry in the areas that became the United States of America just after the American Revolution. We can trace different rituals (or Rites) used worldwide today from early English, French, and other European rituals. Still, for this study, we will confine ourselves to the rituals that are worked in the United States today.

Most craft Masonry in the early United States came from England, Ireland, or Scotland. While variations in these rituals existed, they all came from the same source. Freemasons in the young United States began reorganizing Freemasonry to suit their likes. Some thought was given to having one Grand Lodge for the entire country. But the final plan was to mirror the example of the organization of the new nation's government, meaning more consideration for the states. With that, one Grand Lodge per state was their choice.

In the years that followed, Freemasonry in the United States began refining its nature and defining what it wanted from each Grand Lodge. The consensus was that each Grand Lodge should be as near as possible a copy of the other. Each would be sovereign and independent, yet very similar in the craft lodge experience of the other Grand Lodges. Of course, being sovereign meant that each was free and entitled to operate as they chose best. Over the years, the Masonic craft ritual for most jurisdictions in the US began to vary from a little to a sizable amount, almost defying the original suggested intention.

There seems to have been an early desire for one Grand Lodge per state, one language per Grand Lodge (English), and one ritual for each Grand Lodge. When we try to understand why they wanted the early Grand Lodges organized this way, we cannot look to any ancient charges for answers. The only logical explanation for why they wanted the US Grand Lodges so like each other is because that's what they wanted. Period. Most Masons in the New England states spoke English, so the logical choice was English for the lodges. The decisions of how to model the lodges were based on whatever was in common use for them.

So, with this one Grand Lodge, one language, and one ritual desire, the various Grand Lodges began to organize and refine themselves. Representatives of the various Grand Lodges would meet regularly to discuss the progress of Masonry in the US. But there was a problem for them in South Carolina. To understand the situation in South Carolina, we will need to take a quick look at England. Without getting into a lengthy history of Freemasonry in England, two groups with different Masonic philosophies developed in England before 1800. One styled themselves as the *Ancients* and the other as the *Moderns*. These two Grand Lodges in England were unfriendly towards each other. But they did end up settling their differences and, in 1813, merged into what we have today as the United Grand Lodge of England.[8]

In South Carolina, just before 1800, there were also two Grand Lodges, each representing one of the two styles of English Freemasonry. Both were considered perfectly regular. But the problem remained that the US Grand Lodges' collective desire was for one Grand Lodge per state. Pressure began being placed on South Carolina for these two Grand Lodges to merge. The problem was that they didn't like each other, and they found the others' Masonic philosophy and practice unacceptable. They did not want to merge.[9]

In 1801, a new development and a new problem came with the creation of another Masonic body in South Carolina. This body did not trace itself back to the English style of Freemasonry but to the French style. Throughout the Caribbean islands, a French style of Masonry called the Order of the Royal Secret, more commonly known as the Rite of Perfection, had gained some popularity. This was a 25° system of French-style Masonry that was unique and quite different than the English style of Freemasonry. The problem was that it seemed poorly organized and often lacked clear central leadership.

A group of Masons who had reached the highest degree in this French system met in Charleston, South Carolina, to discuss the problems with this system. Their solution was to create a new system in 1801 with a better organization and central government. The result of this new creation is what we have today as the 33-degree Ancient and Accepted Scottish Rite.

Remember, this new 33° French-style system, like the old 25° system, was a complete system (Masonic Rite) that included its own unique craft degrees. When this new 33°

system was created in Charleston, its "birth certificate" (public announcement) claimed to begin in the craft lodge degrees. But there was an obvious problem. South Carolina was already under considerable pressure because they had two grand bodies controlling craft degrees. The US Grand Lodge community wanted these two bodies to merge so that there would be one. The idea that a *third* body (also controlling craft lodges) would be allowed in that state is unthinkable. For a brand-new organization with tons of potential, this was a deal-breaking problem and one that they needed to address.

While the early records of the Charleston Supreme Council (known commonly today as the *Supreme Council, Southern Jurisdiction* — the Mother Supreme Council of the World) do not exist, we can assume that there was a strong outside objection (or expected objection) to a new body in South Carolina controlling craft degrees. If the young Charleston Council ever did attempt to work in the craft degrees of the Scottish Rite, it would undoubtedly have been short-lived. But we have no information one way or the other. All we know from the existing records is that at some point, the Supreme Council officially confined its degrees from the fourth to the 33rd. There seems to have been an adjustment period and a figuring out of what they would do and how they would operate. It was, after all, a brand-new body and Rite. It seems reasonable that the early Charleston Supreme Council decided to give up their craft lodges in trade for the chance to exist. Without question, if the Charleston Council had insisted on working in or controlling Scottish Rite craft lodges, they would have had a short existence. But outside the United States, the Scottish Rite craft lodge ritual is one of the most popular for well-recognized Grand Lodges in Central America, South America, and Europe.

The Names of the Masonic Degrees are as follow, viz.

1st Degree called, Enter'd Apprentice.
2 —————— Fellow Craft. } Given in the Symbolic Lodge.
3 —————— Master Mason.
4 —————— Secret Master.
5 —————— Perfect Master.
6 —————— Intimate Secretary.
7 —————— Provost and Judge.
8 —————— Intendant of the Building.
9 —————— Elected Knights of 9.
10 —————— Illustrious Elected of 15.
11 —————— Sublime Knight Elected.
12 —————— Grand Master Architect.
13 —————— Royal Arch.
14 —————— Perfection.
15 —————— Knight of the East. } Given by the Princes of Jerufalem, which is a
16 —————— Prince of Jerufalem. } Governing Council.
17 —————— Knight of the East and West.
18 —————— Sovereign Prince of Rofe Croix de Heroden.
19 —————— Grand Pontiff.
20 —————— Grand Master of all Symbolic Lodges.
21 —————— Patriarch Noachite or Chevalier Pruffien.
22 —————— Prince of Lebanus.
23 —————— Chief of the Tabernacle.
24 —————— Prince of the Tabernacle.
25 —————— Prince of Mercy.
26 —————— Knight of the Brazen Serpent.
27 —————— Commander of the Temple.
28 —————— Knight of the Sun.
29 —————— K—M.
30 31 32 —————— Prince of the Royal Secret, Princes of Masons.
33 —————— Sovereign Grand Infpectors General. ————— Officers appointed for Life.

Given in the Sublime Grand Lodge.

Given by the Council of Grand Infpectors, who are Sovereigns of Mafonry.

Befides thofe degrees, which are in regular fucceffion, most of the Infpectors are in poffeffion of a number of detached degrees, given in different parts of the world, and which, they generally communicate, free of expence, to thofe Brethren, who are high enough to understand them. Such as Select Mafons of 27 and the Royal Arch, as given under the Conftitution of Dublin. Six degrees of Maconnerie D'Adoption, Compagnon Ecoffois, Le Maitre Ecoffois & Le Grand Maitre Ecoffois, &c. &c. making in the agregate 52 degrees.

The Committee refpectfully fubmit to the confideration of the Council, the above report on the principles and eftablifhment of the Sublime degrees in South-Carolina, extracted from the archives of the Society. They cannot however conclude, without expreffing their ardent wifhes for the profperity and dignity of the Inftituions over which this Supreme Council prefide; and they flatter themfelves that if any unfavourable impreffions have existed among thefe Brethren of the Blue degrees, from the want of a knowledge of the principles and practices, of Sublime Mafonry, it will be done away, and that harmony and affection, will be the happy cement of the univerfal fociety of Free and Accepted Mafons. That as all aim at the improvement of the general condition of mankind by the practice of virtue, and the exercife of benevolence, fo they fincerely wifh, that any little differences which may have arifen, in unimportant ceremonies of *Ancient* and *Modern*, may be reconciled, and give way to the original principles of the order, thofe great bulwarks of fociety, univerfal benevolence and brotherly love, and that the extenfive fraternity of Free

PLATE 6

*The "Birth Certificate" of the AASR showing the original
Scottish Rite degree names and structure.
Officially titled, "Circular throughout the two Hemispheres"
See: R. Baker Harris and James D. Carter, History of the
Supreme Council, 33° (1801-1861)
(Washington, D.C.: The Supreme Council, 33° Southern
Jurisdiction, USA, 1964) pp. 319-325.*

So, to go back to the beginning of this paper and the current belief among many that the York and Scottish Rites are *appendant bodies*. How did we arrive at that way of thinking? Well, I believe a lack of proper Masonic education and human nature are the leading causes of this misconception and misuse of the term. What do we see if we look at the Scottish Rite in almost all areas of the US? Most experience the Scottish Rite as a 29-degree system. The degrees of the Scottish Rite (from what can be seen by many) span the 4th to 32nd. Many (more than we may assume) view the 33rd degree as an "honorary degree" or award given to some 32nds. They do not see the 33rd as a "real" degree of the Scottish Rite. They know about the supreme council but view it as more of an administrative body. The York Rite is seen as a collection of loosely associated, independent bodies given the general term of "York Rite." Most view the "craft lodge" as an independent entity of no particular "Rite" — it is just "the craft lodge." Both the Scottish Rite and the York Rite are viewed as *organizations* that a Master Mason can join if he wishes. For many years (and, in my opinion, the source of much confusion), it was *necessary* for one with a desire to join the Shriners to first join either the York Rite or Scottish Rite. The York and Scottish Rites held no deeper meaning or importance than being a stepping stone.

Of course, in way too many cases, if we wanted to learn about Scottish Rite history, a good portion of what we received was the near endless (and pointless) arguments to try and show why one Mason, Joseph Cerneau, was irregular and his Scottish Rite was not a "real" Scottish Rite (as well as wholly undesirable and worthless). In the end, no matter which side you fell on in the "Cerneau regularity question," it provided *no* help at all in understanding the profoundly beautiful philosophy of the Scottish Rite. If Joseph Cerneau were 100% regular and a saint of a Mason, it would change nothing as to the importance of the Scottish Rite any more than if he was the devil's own child. I am not saying that Scottish Rite history is unimportant, but I believe it needs to be studied after understanding the philosophy.

Scottish Rite craft lodges in the US became somehow (and incorrectly) tied to "Cerneau Masonry" and viewed as "irregular Masonry" simply because that is what some said of them. Young Masons were molded into believing that the Scottish Rite is a 29-degree system and that Scottish Rite craft lodges should not be allowed to exist. So, these lodges (in the US) were forgotten by some and unknown by others. In time, these young Masons were the senior Masons, and the unfortunate innovation became accepted as law. It is profoundly misleading, uninformed, and dangerous to view the foundation of such an important and beautiful system as the Ancient and Accepted Scottish Rite as irregular and unworthy of use.

And what of the York Rite? Albert Mackey bluntly states:

"In the United States, it has been the almost universal usage to call the Masonry there practiced the York Rite. But it has no better claim to this designation than it has to be called the Ancient and Accepted Rite, or the French Rite, or the Rite of Schroder. It has no pretensions to the York Rite. Or its first three degrees, the Master's is the mutilated one which took the Masonry of England out of the York Rite, and it has added to these three degrees six others which were never known to the Ancient York Rite, or that which was practiced in England, in the earlier half of the 18th century by the legitimate Grand Lodge. In all my writings for years past, I have ventured to distinguish the Masonry practiced in the United States, consisting of nine degrees, as the "American Rite," a title to which it is clearly and justly titled, as the system is particular to America, and is practiced in no other country."[10]

Masonic scholar and historian, Robert Freke Gould, continues in this line of thought with:

"What is commonly known and described as the American Rite, consists of nine degrees, viz.: 1–3, Entered Apprentice, Fellow Craft, and Master Mason, which are given in Lodges, and under the control of Grand Lodges; 4–7, Mark Master, Past Master, Most Excellent Master, and Royal Arch, which are given in Chapters, and under the control of Grand Chapters; 8, 9, Royal Master, and Select Master, which are given in Councils and under the control of Grand Councils. To these, perhaps, should be added three more degrees, namely, Knight of the Red Cross, Knight Templar, and Knight of Malta, which are given in Commanderies, and under the control of Grand Commanderies."[11]

But what is the current view of the York Rite, and which degrees are considered part of the York Rite? From the website titled "York Rite Freemasonry Official Information."

"The York Rite, or more correctly, the American Rite, is based on the early remnants of Craft Masonry that were practiced in the early 1700's. […] Thus, unlike the Ancient and Accepted Scottish Rite, which claims to hold the power of conferring the first three degrees of Masonry in addition to those under its jurisdiction, those found in the York Rite have rightfully acknowledged the fact that they are considered appendant to those of Ancient Craft Masonry."[12]

What does this mean? Let's look at it.

At some point, the York Rite seems to have "forgotten" (or disowned) its craft lodges. During the late 1900s, the York Rite seemed to disconnect itself from the craft lodge, with its membership open to Master Masons. With this, the craft lodge, the York Rite, and the Scottish Rite became three separate entities, with both *Rites* somehow becoming "appendant" to the "craft lodge." But, to which Rite did the craft lodge belong? None? Interesting explanations began to develop. Look again at what is written on this website about how some today view the York Rite and how some compare it with the Scottish Rite,

"… unlike the Ancient and Accepted Scottish Rite, which claims to hold the power of conferring the first three degrees of Masonry in addition to those under its jurisdiction."

What? There are no Masonic *Rites* holding "the power of conferring" any of the degrees of Masonry. Masonic *bodies*, not Rites, hold such power. A Masonic Rite is simply a collection of similar rituals. This is, clearly, the heart of the misunderstandings. It is a twisting up of Masonic *Rites* and Masonic *bodies*. At some point, the term "Rite" became confused with "body," and when speaking of the "Scottish Rite" or "York Rite," it came to be understood to mean certain Masonic bodies or organizations. This is a truly misleading and altogether incorrect understanding of the terms.

Pamphlet published in the 1950s by the "Education Bureau General Grand Chapter, R.A.M" and used until around the 1970s showing the degrees of the "American or York Rite" including the craft lodges degrees. Thanks to Taylor Nauta for the photo.

A Masonic body is an organization that works (labors) in degrees of a Masonic Rite. A Masonic Rite is a collection of similar rituals that begins with the Entered Apprentice Degree (craft degrees) — nothing more, nothing less. Certain Masonic bodies control certain Masonic degrees. A Scottish Rite Lodge of Perfection does not confer the Master Mason degree of its own Rite any more than a York Rite Chapter confers the York Rite Master Mason degree. A *craft lodge* confers the Master Mason degree of *every* Rite. But then again, a Scottish Rite Lodge of Perfection does not have the authority on its own to confer the 33rd degree any more than a York Rite Chapter confers the Knight Templar degree. Certain Masonic bodies control and confer certain degrees regardless of the Rites being worked. The craft lodge degrees (of any Rite) are conferred in craft lodges and in no other bodies. In the early days of US Freemasonry, it was agreed that craft lodges would be under the jurisdiction of Grand Lodges. (Why this was agreed upon is a question for another paper.) A Grand Lodge is a Masonic body just like the craft lodges under its jurisdictions. The Grand Lodge's ritual in its opening and closing of the Grand Lodge is part of a Masonic Rite, just like the rituals used by the lodges under its jurisdiction.

At some point (maybe born out of the internet's self-indulgent, dubious *wisdom* of Wikipedia), York Rite Masons developed this idea that the "York Rite" begins *following* the Master Mason degree. The "York Rite" became a collection of "independent bodies" and not a collection of related rituals. In the same manner of misunderstanding, Grand Lodges developed the idea that Scottish Rite craft rituals were completely irregular and should never be allowed to be worked by craft lodges under their jurisdiction. Of course, many who held this opinion were perfectly agreeable to receiving the 33rd degree of the Scottish Rite as it was a coveted honor to which they felt wholly entitled. The irony of accepting part of a Masonic system yet rejecting another part of the same system is astonishing.

To go back to Albert Mackey's comment quoted at the beginning of this paper. It may seem that our intelligence and success will be determined by how much we know — how much we read, study, and learn. We are in a most exciting time. Young men do seem to be coming to our doors once again, but they are coming with more questions. They expect reasonable, accurate answers. They read — and more than just the internet. I believe that the next years will determine our ultimate level of success in Freemasonry.

Notes:

1. Albert Mackey, *Reading Masons and Masons Who Do Not Read.*
Originally published in *Voice of Masonry*, June 1875.
2. Albert Mackey, *An Encyclopaedia of Freemasonry and its Kindred Sciences: comprising the whole range of arts, sciences, and literature as connected with the institution.* (New Orleans, LA: Cornerstone Book Publishers, 2015 reprint of 1916 edition), p. 626.
3. Today, the Grand Lodge of Louisiana allows two different craft rituals to be used in lodges under its jurisdiction: the York Rite craft ritual and the Ancient and Accepted Scottish Rite craft ritual. In 1833, the Grand Lodge of Louisiana changed its Constitution to allow three different craft rituals: the York Rite craft ritual, the Ancient and Accepted Scottish Rite craft ritual, and the French or Modern Rite craft ritual. In 1850, the Grand Lodge of Louisiana again changed its Constitution to allow only York Rite craft rituals to be worked by its lodges. A period of extreme disarray followed, resulting in the Grand Lodge modifying its Constitution to allow a limited number of lodges to work in the Scottish Rite craft ritual. The French or Modern Rite was not revived under the Grand Lodge of Louisiana. However,

elements of the ritual may have blended into a few of the Scottish Rite craft lodges.

4. Considerable debate exists over the use of "York Rite" to identify any of the rituals or degrees in the US identifying themselves as "York Rite." Albert Mackey led an effort to change the term "York Rite" in the US to "American Rite." His effort was not wholly successful, and today "York Rite" and/or "American Rite" is sometimes used, often leading to confusion with new Masons. Albert Mackey was strongly opposed to using the term "York Rite" for the rituals used in the United States. Others were not so firm against its use. Henry Coil says, "It was quite natural and reasonable that the term, *York Rite*, came by common usage to describe both in Britain and America the Craft agrees with the Royal Arch and later the Knights Templar Degree, together with associated degrees of Mark, Past and Most Excellent Master, the Red Cross and Knight of Malta." Henry Wilson Coil, Allen E. Roberts — Editor, Revised Edition. *Coil's Masonic Encyclopedia* (Richmond, VA: Macoy Publishing & Masonic Supply Co., Inc., 1995) p. 560.

5. This question assumes that Fraternal Relations exist between the bodies. When a Master Mason desires to visit another lodge of Master Masons, and it is outside of his jurisdiction (Grand Lodge), then Fraternal Relations must exist before visitation. Your Grand Secretary can determine if recognition exists between various jurisdictions.

6. Mackey, *An Encyclopaedia of Freemasonry* p. 626.

7. Each jurisdiction's rules and laws of visitation and recognition apply.

8. Mackey, *An Encyclopaedia of Freemasonry* p. 815

9. Ibid., 701. *Coil's Encyclopedia*, p. 626-628. Robert Freke Gould, *A Concise History of Freemasonry*. (New Orleans, LA: Cornerstone Book Publishers, 2020 reprint of 1903 edition), p. 421.

10. Mackey, *An Encyclopaedia of Freemasonry* p. 871.

11. Gould, *A Concise History*. p. 424.

12. See: (https://yorkrite.org/wp/what-is-a-york-rite-mason/) Accessed 12/04/2022.

An Appreciation of Symbolic Art

I recently read a piece on archaeologists discovering cave art of three wild pigs in a limestone cave on the Indonesian island of Sulawesi. They have dated the art at being placed on the cave wall at least 45,500 years ago. Can you imagine that? Can you imagine what was going on at the time this unknown artist painted those images? What was his life like? What did he see around him? What were his thoughts? The questions are endless.

The most common subject of cave art is animals, mostly large animals. Hand tracings and images of humans hunting wild animals of all sorts are common. In still other caves, abstract patterns, called finger flutings, have been found. Finger fluting is when ancient cave dwellers would use their fingers to create lines and patterns in soft sediments that lined the walls and ceilings of the limestone caves. Finger flutings can be simple lines or complex patterns. But how and why was all this created?

Cave paintings were created by mixing (among other things) rocks of various colors, beeswax, animal blood & fat, charcoal, berries, and plant oils. These ingredients would be ground, heated over a fire, and mixed well. The "paint" would then be applied to the cave walls by fingers or twigs chewed down on the end to fashion a primitive paintbrush. They discovered how to create different shades and colors for their paintings through experimentation.

As to why ancient humans created these types of art, well, why do we create and appreciate art today? There are many reasons. Life and death could be quick for early humans. A successful hunt that brought back a good deal of food was something for them to celebrate. So, the guy who could draw recorded the event on the wall. Just like we take pleasure in a painting or photograph of some beautiful place we have visited or would like to visit, maybe they enjoyed remembering the "good hunt." Maybe seeing the animal or hunters in the act of taking down their meal on the wall of their cave brought back good memories. Looking at any images or designs on the wall was likely enjoyable for them, as it is for us today. It doesn't have to mean more than that.

But, in time, some art developed into forms of communication. It is possible that early line art evolved into written language. No one is certain. Certainly, some images were placed on walls or places to be seen as signals of warning or notice about something. But structured, written language is generally (and arguably) said to have begun about 5,500 years ago around Mesopotamia (present-day Iraq). Language and communication, however, can be different things.

Archaeologists have shown that early humans hunted large animals in groups using coordinated attack tactics. To hunt in that manner, they needed to be able to communicate with each other. It is possible that their communications were limited to grunts, yells, and hand gestures. But, to hunt in the way they hunted, it was necessary for them to know what the others would do and for others to know what they would do. Without a language, they still communicated. They did something and others knew what it meant.

While written language was invented over 5,000 years ago, how many people actually used it? Some studies show that as late as the early 1700s, the literacy rate in Europe was as low as 30%. By 1800, it was still only about 50%. Studies also show that in rural areas, it was even lower. If that many could not read, how did they go about day-to-day life? Well, let's say someone was traveling and came into a town. They needed a place to stay for the night. On the sign of a building was the word "Inn." That's the place! But how would they know what that meant if they could not read? They knew because below the word was the image of a bed. Need a place to eat? The sign for that might include eating utensils or a plate of food. A tavern might have a mug of ale on the sign. These were very much forms of communication that provided important information to people, but they were not words. They were symbols. Without the use of written language, information was provided and received.

As Freemasons, we know well how symbols are used to educate our members. We use common images to represent moral lessons. But we were not the only ones.

The Renaissance ushered in a new world of symbolic communications through European art and literature. Enlightenment was the demand of the people. While kings, emperors, and religious leaders desired ignorance of the masses (ignorant masses are far easier to control), the people wanted Light! The problem for the people was that if they displeased the rulers, they could face imprisonment or even, in some cases, horrible deaths. They then turned to symbolic communications.

During the Renaissance, everyday things in life took on dual meanings. Animals, fish, birds, flowers, foods, and more have been used as symbols of things or ideas that would be disapproved of by the controlling powers. Colors played a significant role in symbolic messages, as did clothing, jewelry, shoes (or barefoot), and background settings. Art from the Renaissance period and beyond was filled to the brim with messages hidden in plain sight. Artists could communicate thoughts about religion, politics, or any aspect of life through art and remain out of trouble.

In the early days of Speculative Freemasonry, much of what was discussed in lodges would be acted harshly upon, and this is clearly a reason why so much of our teachings were accomplished using symbolism. If we look at what has become known as "Masonic art," we can discover that many of our teachings are represented by items and images that should not mean anything beyond common, meaningless items for workers. They become much more because they have been used in conjunction with private symbolic interpretations. So, the next time you look at a piece of art (Masonic or not), look a little closer at it. Why is blue used? Why are the hands held in those positions? Why is this door the only one open? It may mean more than you imagine. I hope this paper inspires you to dig deeper into this subject. You may find hidden gold.

Freemasonry: A Magical Order?

Not long ago, I saw a few online posts discussing current anti-Masonic activity. Mostly, it's the same old charges, but maybe with fresh coats of paint. We hear, "Freemasonry is an unacceptable group of unacceptable people who do unacceptable things." Those who are "good Christians" (defined by a small, close-minded group) should stay far away from Freemasonry because it is "anti-Christian." Many of the same, long ago disproven charges are rehashed before a new audience. Conspiracy theory is a key element in this new series of attacks (but even that's hardly new). We hear again that Freemasons control everything and everyone. We use "magical" ceremonies to brainwash our impressionable new members. And Santa is a fat, old elf with a big bag of goodies. We know the story.

Let's look at one element of the anti-Masonic charges — the word "magic" — and explore how it is used today as well as in the past. Let's examine how this word has played a role in accusations against Freemasonry.

Can you imagine stepping into a time machine and returning to, say, the Middle Ages? There you are, standing in a crowd of people, and then, somehow, your cell phone starts ringing. How do you believe the people around you would react? Humans evaluate and respond to situations based on their experiences. We all have heard cell phones ring and someone answering a call. It's a common event. We probably don't even notice someone on the phone. But how would someone in the Middle Ages, with their life experiences, view such an event? You would probably be seen as a wizard who was using supernatural powers. How could you talk with someone who was not standing there with you? Those around you would have no idea what you were doing or how you were doing it. It would likely scare the daylights out of anyone who saw you. Cell phones did not exist in the Middle Ages. Nothing like them existed. They would have been viewed as something impossible to possess. It would be a *magical* device. You would likely be attacked.

During the Middle Ages, whatever was viewed as existing beyond the ordinary or everyday life was dangerous, magical, and, of course, evil. It was the only way that they could explain such things. Magic was anything not understood, and if the Church did not clearly approve something, it must be immoral. A stigma became attached to the word *magic*. It was a stigma born out of ignorance and fear. Today, many with limited understanding of the word *magic* relegate it to two categories: 1) stage entertainment, such as card tricks or making a rabbit pop out of a hat, and 2) malicious groups or individuals using mystical "powers" to engage in morally offensive acts. What we understand or know about something magical is key to how we often view it. You might not know how a magician performs some magic act on a stage, but you know it is a trick. You know that it is not "real magic." It's innocent amusement. You like it because it trips that *how did that happen* switch in you. You still, however, have the safety net of knowing that there is a logical answer and solution. But when something happens that you cannot draw on any personal experience or source to explain you are often left wholly without answers. This type of unexplainable "magical" event or situation triggers fear in some. That's when "magic" can mistakenly be viewed as wicked, immoral, and evil.

Claude Bernard tells us, "Man can learn nothing except by going from the known to the unknown." Even when we consider the powerful fear of the unknown, our human quest for knowledge has always existed and was never, for long, denied. We were and are curious beings. In the early days of humanity, lightning striking a tree must have been a terrifying event. How could anyone understand such a sight and sound? The tree must have been viewed as dangerous long after the strike. But this would not have stopped a curious few from approaching the "dangerous" tree and touching it. Maybe they could not answer why they did such a foolish thing, but they *had* to do it. They *had* to reach out.

The end of the Dark Ages was an ignorant, violent, and fearful time. If you did something to create fear in another, you would most likely face harm — and fear of magic or the unknown was a profound fear. The dawn of the Middle Ages saw the Church as the accepted source (by force) of all legitimate information, knowledge, and answers. Anyone seeking answers for what was not explained by the Church put their very lives in danger — *by* the Church. Yet some did just that. They questioned information or answers provided by the Church. They sought to learn for themselves and reach beyond the restricted teachings of the Church. They knowingly sought knowledge at the risk of their lives. They *had* to do it. They *had* to reach out. These Seekers of Light gave birth to what we know today as mysticism and esoterism, but also medicine, science, and a host of other well-respected fields. In the words of Albert Einstein, "The most beautiful thing we can experience is the mystical. It is the source of all true art and science."

Esoteric knowledge or teachings were private or inner teachings that were never made available to everyone. In most all cases, these teachings were carefully guarded as to be associated with them could bring an actual death sentence. Small groups of students would secretly gather to explore deeper aspects of themselves and their world. Vows and oaths were often required of members in such groups to protect them and better the chance of the continuation of the group. The seeds of what we have today as Freemasonry were sown in this atmosphere.

When the little groups of knowledge seekers illegally gathered, they could not speak or teach freely. Even within their group, they could not provide open educational material out of concern that it would be discovered and result in imprisonment or death. So, they employed the use of symbols. This was not, at all, a new way of teaching. Communicating valuable or confidential information by symbols has been in use since the dawn of humanity. And it was always effective. The use of symbols could offer profound education, and yet those uninitiated in the meanings of the symbols would be able to see nothing of what was, in reality, being taught. It was not only a useful way to instruct, but it provided security.

Freemasonry teaches by employing symbols because its roots are in the esoteric groups that used this method to teach. Esoterism is not a foreign subject to Freemasonry. It is as much a part of Freemasonry's fabric as initiation. But look at all that has changed around us since the Middle Ages. Yes, how Freemasonry teaches its initiates to be more valuable members of society is the same as how it was taught in the past, but society has profoundly changed. Education is now a central part of society. Science, mathematics, medicine, and so on are not only allowed to be taught to our young, but foundational schooling is required of them. We not only allow education but require it for our children because we know that an educated population is a more valuable and beneficial society. An ignorant society can be better controlled, but if we are truly free, then education of all benefits everyone, and we know it. We want a knowledgeable population because we know it better serves all of us.

Even though many do not agree on the origins of Freemasonry, we can trace what we have today back to a time when education was not as open and accessible. Freemasonry offered a source of actual enlightenment to many who were denied such teachings elsewhere in society. Freemasonry was also painted with the same brush as other groups of "unsanctioned instruction." In the eyes of the peddlers of falsehood, we became immoral and wholly unacceptable to the "true followers of Christianity." It is complete nonsense and ignorant lies, but it is the foundation and essence of the anti-Masonic movement. Calculated deceptions are the weapons and tools of those who would use selected, financially modified religion to control the hearts and minds of others. True faith is not self-serving, bigoted, nor blind.

Magic is a word used to describe something seen but not completely understood. If we are "magical" because we initiate our candidates, then so be it. If we are "magical" because we do not limit our members to only those defined as "Christian" by anti-Masonic perverters of the truth, then so be it. As a Freemason, I openly and freely confess that I refuse to judge the religious faiths of my brothers. The teachings of Freemasonry are designed to help all its members live better lives in service of the Creator and humanity. We use symbols in our manner of instruction because we have done so since a time when such education was punished by those intent on denying true Light to others. We are proud of what we teach and how we teach it. If all this means that Freemasons are "magical," well, I am honored to be a magician.

Why Didn't Hiram Fight Back?

I've written more than a few papers on the legend of Hiram. The reason for returning to this subject so often is because this legend presents the Masonic instruction of integrity so brilliantly. Like all great symbolic lessons, the Hiramic Legend can also be viewed from different angles. In one viewing, we see one example, and in another, we see something very different but equally important.

Not long ago, I received an interesting question. I was asked if I believed that Hiram needed to die to teach anything about integrity. The brother questioned if the lesson of integrity would have been compromised if Hiram had refused to give them what they wanted but still fought back to save his life. Well, no, I don't believe that the moral would be compromised, but let's look at this question.

To start with, it should again be pointed out that this is a work of fiction. There is no evidence that this story of Hiram is an actual historical account. Masonry offers it as a vehicle to teach symbolic moral lessons. But any symbolic lesson worth anything has layers of lessons that can be drawn from it — even ones that were not originally written into it.

So, if we take the legend at face value, then Hiram was the Grand Master of a group of Operative Freemasons. We can take this to mean that he was a highly skilled Operative Freemason. He would have worked his way up from an apprentice. Then he would have, based on his overall skill, been selected as the leader of all the Masters — the Grand Master.

Hiram's work and path would have been long and hard. He would likely have been middle-aged or a bit past middle-aged to reach the point he reached. He most likely spent most of his life doing strenuous physical labor from sun up to sun down.

As to the three "bad guys," well, they were not yet Masters. They were young and undoubtedly in good physical shape from years of hard work. They were not inexperienced apprentices. They were Fellows of the Craft.

While there is no suggestion that Hiram was feeble, he was certainly not in the same physical shape he was in during his youth. To take on three young men in their prime might have been a lot to expect from him. But, on the other hand, while Hiram was older and no longer in the same physical shape that he once was, why, indeed, would he not at least put up some fight against individuals who threatened to kill him? This is where symbolic moral lessons come into play.

A quality leader is always looking for those who can replace him. The only way that any organization or group can keep existing over the years is to have a constant stream of quality leaders with the organization's best interests at heart. Those leaders who only look out for their own best interests are the cancer within any group. The power-hungry, ego-driven leader is the weak link in any chain, regardless of any bravado they might display. So, how does a quality leader look for his replacements?

Elite military or law enforcement leaders often come up through the ranks and undergo extensive training. I watched something on military training recently, and it caught my attention. It was a Navy SEAL talking about leaders and an event during a training operation when he was one of the new guys. It was training that they had participated in many times before. They were to clear a building.

Everyone in this training exercise was focused on what they were doing and the next steps they would take. A threat could pop up anywhere and anytime. They came into a room and were all looking down the barrels of their weapons and waiting for the instructor to give the next call. They waited. And they waited longer. But no instructions came.

The group of trainees began to realize that they were waiting too long, doing nothing. In an actual combat situation, this could be a problem. Finally, this new guy couldn't stand it any longer. He knew something was wrong. He then did something on his own.

The new guy pointed his weapon at the ceiling and moved back just a couple of inches. Then he looked around. He could see his platoon commander, the assistant commander, and everyone else, all frozen, looking down the barrel of their weapons. He then looked around at the whole area. He could see what needed to be done because of his taking a step back and looking at the whole situation. But no one gave the call.

Calling up his courage, he yelled out: "Hold Left! Clear Right!"

It was a basic command they had done many times before and one he knew was correct for this situation. He expected someone to yell back, "Shut up! Who are you?!" Instead, he heard the command repeated, and they began executing just like they had done so many times. When it was over, he said that he fully expected one of the senior guys to chew him out for stepping out of line, but they just came up and told him, "Good job stepping up."

You see, it was a test. The point was that a leader or leaders giving the commands could be taken out at any moment. What happens to the team after that? If no one steps up, then they all may be lost. This test was to find potential future leaders. They needed to see who would first step up and then, second, give the correct call.

There is a lesson here for us all.

We don't need leaders in Freemasonry who don't know what they are doing. All the ego and loud talk in the world does not replace knowledge of Freemasonry. We also don't need leaders who fear stepping up, even when things are difficult. A leader must have the courage to do the right thing, even when he may be risking it all.

From just these points, Hiram would have displayed all the qualities of a true quality leader. According to what we know, Hiram displayed tremendous courage when facing those who would end up murdering him. He didn't give them what they wanted. He didn't violate his promises.

But the story does not tell us if he put up any fight to save his life. That may not be necessary to the story, but it is an interesting question. Let's try to find out if there could be more to this story.

Hiram may not have had great personal knowledge of the three bad guys, but we can assume that he at least knew them. He knew that they were not among the ones slated for advancement. If we delve into the realm of all things possible, then upon first seeing them, Hiram may have desired to test them further.

There is no clear answer with Hiram because the situation is not addressed in the story. All we can do is try to build on what we know and don't know. The test for the Navy SEALS was for the leader to do nothing at all so that he may see who steps up and does the right thing.

Hiram was a quality leader. He would have always been looking for those who could fill the leadership shoes in the future. While it's not explained why Hiram acted and did not act in certain ways during this confrontation, it is a fascinating study of human nature. I don't have any obvious or provable answers to the question, but it is not impossible that Hiram's last moments alive were to think of the welfare of the Order from more than one position.

Hiram may have hoped that the bad guys could be redeemed at the last moment. It didn't happen, but it would show a unique quality in Hiram that he never gave up hope in his workers, even when hope was a very long shot. It would display a unique kindness and unyielding loyalty to the members.

From this story's outcome, we know that all tested are not worthy. Unworthy craftsmen need to be identified and kept from our inner circles. When given every chance, some will consistently choose the wrong path. They will put themselves and their own best interest first. But Hiram chose the right path from every way you view this situation.

The story is worth looking at and thinking about over and over. These moral lessons contain hidden gems that we may only find with a close examination. As with so very many of the Masonic symbolic lessons, you only need to study them a bit.

A Family Split and Forgotten
The Craft Lodges of the AASR

In 1857, two years before he was elected Sovereign Grand Commander, Albert Pike was elected to the office of Commander in Chief of the Grand Consistory of Louisiana in New Orleans.[1] In his Inaugural Address, ordered to be printed in the Minutes of the Grand Consistory, he said in part: "My brethren, I see around me the representatives of more than one race, and the disciples of more than one Masonic Rite — I rejoice at this reunion, and it gives me happy augury of the prosperity, health, and continuance of Masonry in this Valley."[2] That's an interesting statement. Let's look at it. While it is impossible to get into the mind of someone dead for almost 150 years, we can find several significant elements in what he said. First, what does Albert Pike mean by "representatives of more than one race"? Is he saying that this meeting in 1857 was *not* limited to only Caucasian Masons? That could be true as race was not the issue in New Orleans that it became in later years. There were Black and racially mixed Masons in New Orleans in the early to mid-1800s, but I am not entirely sure that this is what he meant.

Early New Orleans was French by language and culture. Before Pike could practice law in New Orleans (his reason for going to the city), he needed to prove that he could read and write in French.[3] This was because French was the language of most old New Orleans legal records. The French and Creoles[4] in New Orleans were often referred to as being of the "Latin race." Pike could have used the word "race" to speak of the French and Creoles in the Grand Consistory. Without more context, it is not completely clear what Pike meant by his use of the word.

It is, however, the second part of that statement that I would especially like to look at in this paper. Albert Pike said, "I see around me […] the disciples of more than one Masonic Rite." What does he mean? Certainly, Pike did not mean that York Rite Masons, who were not also members of the Scottish Rite, were attending a meeting of the Grand Consistory of Louisiana. Pike may have merely been acknowledging those Masons who belonged to both rites. But that does not make sense when you consider what he said next. Pike stated, "I rejoice at this reunion, and it gives me happy augury of the prosperity, health, and continuance of Masonry in this Valley." What reunion? There was no conferral of degrees that day. It sounds as if he is saying there was a rejoining of those who were once separated. Is there some suggestion that, for a time, members of the Scottish Rite in Louisiana were not allowed to be members of the York Rite (or vice-versa)? I've seen no evidence to support any such ban. At least, I've seen no evidence of problems at that time with established Masonic rites or rituals *above* the craft degrees. When speaking of craft degrees, however, a near Masonic war existed in Louisiana just ten years before Pike's speech over the rituals used in the New Orleans area craft lodges. The rituals used in these craft lodges were still a very emotional subject in 1857. I believe that Pike's comment had to do with craft Masonry and the meeting together again of Masons belonging to lodges using various craft lodge rituals. From the early days of Freemasonry in Louisiana and for only a short time following 1850, lodges under the jurisdiction of the Grand Lodge of Louisiana worked in several craft lodge rituals — different Masonic rites. Louisiana is a unique situation in US Freemasonry.

The city of New Orleans was founded in 1718 by Jean Baptiste Le Moyne de Bienville. The earliest known record of Freemasonry in New Orleans is July 16, 1752, when the lodge la Parfaite Harmonie was created.[5] This was a French-styled lodge created by Masons arriving in New Orleans from the West Indies. This lodge, and the ones that followed, would have worked in the language of the members, and used the Masonic rituals that were commonly available to them. In this case, it would have been French language lodges working in the rituals they brought with them from the West Indies (or France). These early French rituals would evolve into what we have today as the Ancient and Accepted Scottish Rite and the French or Modern Rite craft rituals. Before the Louisiana Territory would become a territory of the United States, it would exist under the jurisdiction of France, Spain, and then again, for a short time, France. Freemasonry in New Orleans (just as the people and culture) was very different than in any other area of what would become the United States. It was as if it were a separate and distinct nation with its customs and practices.

The two oldest existing lodges in New Orleans are Perfect Union No. 1, created in 1793, and Etoile Polaire No. 1, created in 1794.[6] Both of these lodges work today in English, but initially, they each worked in the French language.

Additionally, Perfect Union is known as the oldest "York Rite" (American Webb ritual) lodge and Etoile Polaire as the oldest "Scottish Rite" (AASR craft ritual) lodge. The problem is that neither of their present-day rituals existed in the mid-1790s.[7] They would have worked in older rituals. Another problem is that many of these lodges' early records and documents were lost or destroyed. After years of research, no original rituals attributed to these lodges have turned up. It seems most likely that they used existing rituals of the old, so-called Rite of Perfection (Order of the Royal Secret) or whatever rituals they had available.

In 1803, the United States purchased the Louisiana Territory from France. The Louisiana Territory was approximately 827,000 square miles and nearly doubled the physical size of the United States. The jewel of the Louisiana Purchase was the valuable Port of New Orleans. Merchants in the US often found it far cheaper and safer to bring their goods down the Mississippi River to the Port of New Orleans. Once in New Orleans, they could ship from the Gulf of Mexico to almost anywhere. Along with merchandise, these riverboats brought visitors, including Masons, to the city of New Orleans.

While Freemasonry in Louisiana suffered during the Spanish control of Louisiana (either disappearing or going underground), it flourished as a territory of the United States. While continuing to be French in language and culture, New Orleans welcomed those of different backgrounds. The city became a melting pot of diverse people. Freemasonry was no different. Lodges of foreign languages, rituals, and cultures found a home in the New Orleans Masonic community. But more than craft Masonry was welcomed in Louisiana. In 1811, a Grand Consistory of the AASR was established in New Orleans under the jurisdiction of Alexandre de Grasse's 1804 Supreme Council in Kingston, Jamaica. This Grand Consistory has a remarkable and often controversial Masonic history. It changed jurisdictions, nature, and structure numerous times. Masonic historians would make a grave mistake in believing that its history is entirely or accurately understood. The current Valley of New Orleans traces itself (probably, but not 100% proven) back to this 1811 body.[8]

On April 30, 1812, Louisiana became the 18th state in the United States of America. Less than two months later, on June 20, 1812, five French-speaking New Orleans lodges elected the first Grand Master of the Grand Lodge of Louisiana. Many of the founding members of the Grand Lodge were also members of the 1811 Grand Consistory of Louisiana. Like the rituals of the early New Orleans lodges, the original rituals of the Grand Lodge of Louisiana have not been identified. But it is known that they were French language rituals, which would likely be the same ones used by the lodges.

In time, the older French rituals seemed to have fallen out of favor, and the French Masons of New Orleans began moving to either the French or Modern Rite or the Scottish Rite craft rituals. The Grand Lodge operated more along the lines of the European Grand Lodges. The Grand Lodge did not involve itself in what seemed to be "lodge only" matters, such as the language of the lodge or the rituals in which the lodge chose to work. As long as it was a valid Masonic ritual that was worked somewhere by a legitimate Masonic body, it was felt acceptable for Louisiana lodges.

The city of New Orleans began to grow mainly due to its port and the traffic it brought to the city. Masons coming into the city and desiring to visit local lodges were often startled by the Masonry practiced in this French city. Freemasonry in most areas of the US was English-speaking and, for the most part, worked the Preston-Webb style of ritual. The French language and rituals used by the New Orleans lodges were unfamiliar. The general feeling of the visitors was that they did not like or approve of this type of Freemasonry.

The Grand Lodge of Louisiana sought to accommodate their lodges by issuing charters to lodges working in the language and ritual of their choice. Over the years, charters have been given to lodges working in French, English, Spanish, Italian, and German. But the rituals used by the lodges seemed to be at the top of the "problem list" for some English-speaking Masons coming into New Orleans. By the 1830s, hot-blooded disputes over the legitimacy of the various rituals were levied against the French-speaking lodges. In an attempt to clarify and resolve the situation, the Grand Lodge of Louisiana, in 1833, officially acknowledged, through charters and concordats, the "York Rite" (American-Webb), the French or Modern Rite, and the "Scotch"[9] Rite (AASR) craft rituals. The lodges would only need to inform the Grand Lodge which ritual they desired to work, and the Grand Lodge would issue them the appropriate charter. The Grand Lodge believed this would accommodate everyone and settle any perceived legitimacy issues concerning the rituals. The Grand Lodge greatly misread the intentions of the English-speaking Masons.

Instead of solving the problems, the English-speaking Masons were infuriated by the 1833 actions of the Grand Lodge.[10] The English-speaking Masons felt that since Louisiana was a part of the United States, the Grand Lodge of Louisiana should limit itself to only English-speaking lodges. They also felt that the lodges should work in *only* the Preston-Webb ritual. They believed this was the ritual (or a version) used by all other US lodges. The Grand Lodge put its foot down. It felt that the English-speaking Masons were being unreasonable. The Grand Lodge tried to explain that the city did not have a single language, and many senior Masons knew only French (or other languages), and they had worked in the rituals their lodge used for many years. They pointed to the many European Grand Lodges, which worked in multiple rituals. But the English-speaking Masons were firm. They felt that any deviation from English-speaking lodges working in the Preston-Webb ritual in the US was a deviation from regular Freemasonry.

Regardless of if the English-speaking Masons were being reasonable or unreasonable, the Grand Lodge of Louisiana could foresee trouble. While once the French-speaking population was in the overwhelming majority, that number was, however, whittled down with the influx of a steady stream of English-speaking transplants (including Masons) into New Orleans. This was due to the ease of travel into the city from the Mississippi River. And then things exploded.

In 1845, a handful of New Orleans area English-speaking Masons, led by New Orleans attorney and Mason John Gedge, petitioned the Grand Lodge of Mississippi for relief. They claimed that the Grand Lodge of Louisiana was not regular as they issued charters to craft lodges working in the Scottish Rite and French or Modern Rite craft rituals. The years between then and Pike's speech were a devastating ten or so years for Louisiana Freemasonry.[11]

The Grand Lodge of Mississippi moved slowly but ultimately sided with Gedge and his splinter group, declaring the Grand Lodge of Louisiana irregular and open territory. By early 1848, The Grand Lodge of Mississippi had chartered seven lodges in and around New Orleans. The same year these lodges organized themselves into a second Grand Lodge, *The Louisiana Grand Lodge of Ancient York Rite Masons*, and elected John Gedge as its Grand Master. While no other Grand Lodge, save the Grand Lodge of Mississippi, recognized this new Grand Lodge (and a number condemned it), the Grand Lodge of Louisiana could see serious trouble on the horizon.

Freemasonry has always been inclined to mirror the society where it exists. New Orleans was no different. The French style of Freemasonry in the Grand Lodge of Louisiana reflected the French culture of the city. But this French city and Grand Lodge were becoming American. Many French in the Grand Lodge realized that it was only a matter of time before the English-speaking Masons would outnumber the French. Fearing they would lose everything, they felt that the best path was to negotiate with this new Grand Lodge to see if they could come to terms and possibly merge. By doing this, they felt they could preserve some of their heritage and customs. Negotiations between the two Grand Lodges began, and they did reach an agreement.

On January 28, 1850, the Grand Lodge of Louisiana and the Louisiana Grand Lodge settled and merged the two Grand Lodges into one. The seven lodges created by the Grand Lodge of Mississippi would pass under the jurisdiction of the Grand Lodge of Louisiana. John Gedge, Grand Master of the irregular Louisiana Grand Lodge, would become Grand Master of the Grand Lodge of Louisiana. For a short time, it seemed that the compromise that had been reached would assure peace in Louisiana Masonry. But then Gedge instructed all non-York Rite lodges to turn in their charters so they could receive York Rite charters. Only then did it become clear that the merger that was believed to have taken place was an actual takeover by the Gedge group. The original demands of the English-speaking Masons were being realized. The new Grand Lodge would become English-speaking and work in only the "York Rite" Preston-Webb ritual. Charges of trickery were made, and three lodges withdrew from the new Grand Lodge.[12] The peace that had been hoped for was dashed, and an all-out war began between the two sides.

Louisiana Freemasonry was in a state of turmoil. The divisions in Freemasonry were so pronounced and hostile that it is not an exaggeration to recognize that the sentiments advanced from "I'm right, and you are wrong!" to "I'm good, and you are evil!" After several years, it seemed to be a hopeless situation. The future of Masonry in Louisiana seemed dim. We can only speculate on what might have happened had the open hostilities continued, but then an event occurred that no one could have predicted.

1853 brought the worse yellow fever epidemic on record in New Orleans. Estimates of around 8,000 New

Orleanians died (some a lingering, gruesome death) from this outbreak. Masonic losses during this outbreak included John Gedge and a large portion of the pro-Gedge Grand Lodge of Louisiana line. The 1853 to 1855 *Proceedings* of the Grand Lodge of Louisiana show amazing events and the toll that the yellow fever epidemic took on the city and Louisiana Freemasonry. Both sides lost indispensable members. The fire seemed to be taken out of the resolve of most all Masons to continue the fighting in the Grand Lodge. Negotiations began again, and compromises were made where no one won all that they wished nor lost all that they feared.

There is little doubt in my mind that the "reunion" that Pike spoke of in his 1857 address before the Grand Consistory of Louisiana was the return of Scottish Rite craft Masons to Louisiana Masonry. While all new charters would be for York Rite lodges, the historic rituals of the Scottish Rite craft lodges were allowed to return to the Grand Lodge of Louisiana. However, the French or Modern Rite rituals did not return and may have blended into some of the Scottish Rite ritual lodges. An uneasy truce was reached.

And that brings us to the present. The handful of Scottish Rite lodges that were allowed to exist in the 1850s have evolved into ten lodges[13] that comprise the 16th District of the Grand Lodge of Louisiana. They are the "Scottish Rite District." They work as a unique, historic, and proud district of the Grand Lodge of Louisiana. Members of these lodges have served the Grand Lodge in all offices, including Grand Master of the Grand Lodge of Louisiana. Many of them have received the 33rd degree of the Southern Jurisdiction, and a number have served as Sovereign Grand Inspectors General of the Supreme Council, SJUSA. Anyone who has seen the rituals of these lodges can verify their beauty and highly symbolic nature. So, why are there so few of these lodges in US Masonry? Let's try to examine that question.

Following the American Revolution, Freemasonry in the very young United States was set up according to the rules made by the Masons of that time. The Almighty did not create and give these rules to the Masons of the United States. Men created the rules. They made rules that they felt would best serve Freemasonry in this country. Many rules seem, however, arbitrary. They were made by Masons who were setting up what they felt should be the norm for Freemasonry in a new land. Decisions were often made without deeper reason or meaning than how they wanted their Masonry to work. It was usually only a continuation of what they knew of Freemasonry. The language of Masonry was English because that was the language of most of the Masons in the new United States. The ritual was a refinement of the ritual used by most US Masons. All was fine, but then the new USA began to grow. When the US obtained the massive Louisiana Territory, New Orleans was included. Freemasonry there was not of the same language, ritual, or culture as in the rest of the US. That presented them with a problem that only grew.

The rituals and languages of Freemasonry in New Orleans were found unacceptable simply because it was not how things were done in the rest of the US. We can find no deeper meaning or reason. There was no thought or consideration for "the way things were done" in New Orleans. Masonry in New Orleans was different. "Different" became viewed as improper…unacceptable. Freemasonry in New Orleans needed to change so that it was no longer *different*. It was a trying time for everyone.

The intolerant attitudes evolved into beliefs that any craft ritual that was not the American-Webb style ritual was considered irregular...unMasonic. They were unacceptable for any US craft lodge. But what about the other rituals of the Ancient and Accepted Scottish Rite? Well, the AASR rituals from the 4th to 33rd were felt to be acceptable. The only problem was with the AASR rituals from the 1st to 3rd degrees. The fact that they were all rituals of the very same system seemed irrelevant. Masons became fixed in their opinions, and nothing would change their minds. Over time, most US Masons forgot the craft lodges of the AASR. It was only those who lived in the New Orleans area or those who visited there and happened to visit one of those "strange lodges" who knew that they existed. Even today, with the advent of the internet, many still have little knowledge of the existence of these lodges. The fact that the AASR craft ritual is one of the most popular rituals in regular recognized Freemasonry outside of the US is often ignored or unknown.

For those in the US who are aware of the AASR craft degrees worked *in* the US, we often find curious beliefs. Some disapprove of these lodges for no other reason than "they are unacceptable and not regular." When pushed for an excuse to justify such a belief, no logical answer can be given — they are simply unacceptable. On the other hand, others almost venerate them and wish these "magnificent lodges" could be in all jurisdictions. Some view them as a *Camelot* where everything is good, fair, and inspired. For others, the lodges are like *Dante's Inferno*, where nothing is proper, helpful, or legal. Why do we have such highly contradictory opinions? What is the truth?

Anyone who has spent time in New Orleans and visited the ten lodges of the 16th District knows that these are like any other lodges in the area (or any area), except that they use a different ritual. Within these ten lodges are strong lodges and ones that are almost on life support. Some lodges do excellent ritual work, and some can barely open. Some are well organized, and some are not. They operate like any ten lodges anywhere else in the US. The only difference is their ritual. Those who expect to see flames shooting out of the eyes of the lodge officers find only normal Masons (ones like they might find in their community) trying to do the work of their lodge. The same is true of those who expect to see perfection in every aspect of the lodge operation. They are often disappointed when they find only "normal Masons" and not "enlightened sages." What is found are Masons with the same strengths and weaknesses as in any other lodge. They are not devils or saints. They are just Masons trying to practice Freemasonry as they learned in their lodge.

Yes, there is a historical aspect to working the Scottish Rite craft lodges in the US. Unfortunately, they are looked at disapprovingly by some. Yet, others greatly admire them. Most US Masons have no opinion at all. The simple fact is that *all* the degrees of the AASR, from EA to SGIG, teach profound, moral, and philosophical lessons. They are *all* beautiful guides for living. They are all worthy of study.

If our goal in the Scottish Rite is to "gain Light" only to "gain importance," then we will fail to understand or grow in philosophical enlightenment. To thrive in the Scottish Rite, we must know the Scottish Rite and all its teachings. We must seek Light to grow in knowledge and internal worth. There is profound wisdom and valuable lessons in the craft degrees of the Scottish Rite because it was designed to be the foundation of the whole system. No great temple is built with a weak, unacceptable, or irregular foundation. If we wish to claim the Scottish Rite, we must correctly understand the whole of the Scottish Rite. This would include an appreciation of the value of the craft degrees of our system.

NOTES:

1. See: Michael R. Poll, "Albert Pike's Address before the Grand Consistory of Louisiana," *Heredom*, vol. 10, (Washington, DC: The Scottish Rite Research Society, 2002) pp. 223-242.
2. Ibid., 234.
3. See https://lasc.libguides.com/c.php?g=457651&p=3181671. Accessed March 4, 2022.
4. The term "Creole" is often understood as applying to race. It was also used in the 1800s in New Orleans to identify one as part of a particular cultural segment. See: Michael R. Poll, "Creole Freemasons of New Orleans," *The Scottish Rite Papers*, (New Orleans, LA: Cornerstone Book Publishers, 2020) pp. 50-65.
5. *Sharp Document #40* is in the Archives of the Supreme Council NMJ USA, Lexington, Massachusetts. See also: *The Sharp Documents*, vol. IV (Rennes, France: The Latomia Foundation, 1993) 1.
6. At the creation of the Grand Lodge of Louisiana, Perfect Union was given the number "1." Etoile Polaire was given the number "5." In 1833, the Grand Lodge of Louisiana began issuing charters to lodges in the rite of their choice. Etoile Polaire kept its York Rite charter but requested a charter for the Scottish Rite and received the number "1." The lodge also asked for and received a French or Modern rite charter. This charter also carried the number "1" (reflective of the 1st charter for a French or Modern rite lodge). The Grand Lodge Proceedings between 1834 and 1841 are lost or destroyed. The 1842 Proceedings show Etoile Polaire with only a Scottish Rite charter and carrying the number "1." No information is available as to why Etoile Polaire turned in its York Rite and French or Modern Rite charters.
7. Perfect Union today works in the Preston-Webb ritual. This ritual was not hammered out until about 1816. There is no record of when

Perfect Union switched to this ritual, but it likely occurred in 1887 when the lodge merged with Marion Lodge #77. This was one of the seven lodges created by the Grand Lodge of Mississippi in 1847-48. It is also likely that this was when they switched to English. While debate exists about the actual creation date (and nature) of the first craft ritual used for the 33-degree AASR, there is no evidence of the ritual used initially by Etoile Polaire. If we set 1801 as the creation date of the AASR in Charleston, then it would be impossible for a lodge in New Orleans to use that ritual seven years before 1801. It would seem more likely that Etoile Polaire used one of the available, older rituals that would have existed in New Orleans or from the West Indies. It is unclear when Etoile Polaire made the actual switch to the AASR craft ritual, but it was clearly by 1833.

8. See: Michael R. Poll, "The Early Years of the Grand Consistory of Louisiana (1811-1815)," *Heredom*, vol. 8, (Washington, DC: The Scottish Rite Research Society, 1999-2000) pp. 39-54. See also: Arturo de Hoyos, "The Early Years of the Grand Consistory of Louisiana (1811-1815) — A Rejoinder," *Heredom*, vol. 9, (Washington, DC: The Scottish Rite Research Society, 2001) pp. 69-102 and Michael R. Poll, "A Few 'Rejoinder' Comments," *Heredom*, vol. 9, (Washington, DC: The Scottish Rite Research Society, 2001) pp. 103-110.

9. The term "Scotch Rite" was often used in early New Orleans when translating the French "Rite Écossais" (Scottish Rite) into English.

10. See: Michael R. Poll, "The Elimination of the French Influence in Louisiana Masonry," *The Scottish Rite Papers*, (New Orleans, LA: Cornerstone Book Publishers, 2020) pp. 22-49.

11. Ibid.

12. Etoile Polaire, Los Amigos Del Orden (today Cervantes), and Disciples of the Masonic Senate (merged with Etoile Polaire in 1895).

13. At the January, 2007 Communications of the Grand Lodge of Louisiana (2007 Proceedings pg. 64) Grand Master Clayton J. Borne, III expanded the number of lodges allowed to work in the AASR craft ritual via Resolution. In addition to the ten lodges of the 16th district, the Grand Lodge would allow one additional lodge from each of the other district to work in this ritual. In 2020, Goose & Gridiron organized to work in the AASR craft

ritual in Alexandria, LA. On May 8, 2021, they received their charter to become Goose & Gridiron No. 1717 assigned to the 20th District. To date, they are the only lodge outside of the 16th district to work in the AASR craft ritual and the 11th AASR craft ritual lodge under the Grand Lodge of Louisiana.

Freemasonry in Leadership Crisis

If we say, "I see" it can mean several different things. It can mean that we visibly observe something, or it can mean that we understand something. We can say, "I see the dog over there" or we can say, "I see what you mean." Many today "see" the problem that Freemasonry faces. The problem is declining members. We don't have the members we once had so that means we don't have the money coming in that we once had. We need to scale back. We can do that. Over the last few decades, we have seen large, historic Masonic temples sold and a downsizing of the infrastructure of a number of Grand Bodies. We have seen more than a few lodge mergers and even lodge failures. But too many do not see a problem that is related to membership loss. This often ignored or unnoticed problem is what I want to cast a light on.

Few will argue that Masonry needs quality leaders. Masonry needs leaders with talent, creative minds, and the ability to get things done. Every single year we need such leaders. With declining membership, this is often a difficult task to bring into reality. It seems that too often we end up settling for whoever is just sitting in the room on election nights. Masonry suffers because we can, at best, only tread water with leaders who are untrained in Masonry and/or lacking in leadership skills. But we seem to get by. Year after year rolls by and if nothing serious happens, we do (most often) survive. We coast along and become accustomed to leaders who not so long ago would have never been allowed to reach the position that they today reach. Past leaders are often present to help if rough waters overwhelm an unskilled leader. Sadly though, past leaders today are often as unskilled as the sitting leaders. Time sometimes does this to Masonic bodies in trouble. But as long as the problems are not to the level of total destruction of the body, we do seem to keep drifting on.

But what I am saying does not mean that quality leaders do not exist. Gems do show up almost out of nowhere. Suddenly, we find a young man with the skill, talent, and drive that brings back memories of "the old days." You bet your boots we grab them and rush them into leadership positions. We want everyone to see how lucky we are to have such a quality Mason in the leadership of our Masonic body! We have found this great young leader and that is proof that Freemasonry in our area is not dead! But it is right here that problems we may not readily see begin to appear.

Yes, the talented young Mason with loads of ability does a good (maybe great) job in this or that body. It has been years since the body has seen such a talented and worthy leader! He is, of course, quickly noticed by other bodies. Soon, everyone is knocking on his door to propose a leadership position in their body. Honors, notoriety, and flattering offers shower down on the young star. He becomes "somebody" very quickly with all the praise and ego boasting words and actions that can be delivered. And then what? What happens to the talented, young Masonic celebrity who everyone wants? That's what many, including the talent young Mason, did not see might happen.

No matter who we are, how talented or gifted we may be, we are still governed by the laws of nature. We all have only 24 hours in our days. No amount of praise or honors thrown at us can change that fact. To all young Masons who receive praise and requests to accept various offices, please stop, think, and read this advice. Take it for what it is worth.

If you accept every offer extended to you, you must realize that the quality of your work will diminish depending on how much is expected of you from everyone. I have personally seen highly talented young Masons burn themselves out trying to help everyone who asked. The truth is that some bodies operate almost on autopilot. All a leader needs to do is show up, handle paying bills, and running simple business meetings. The problem is that you never know when something serious will happen that requires a leader to do *far* more than just open and close meetings. It is here that a truly talented leader can be of service to Masonry. But if that talented leader is already handling duties or problems in multiple bodies, then he may face exhaustion and be able to properly handle nothing. Far more damage can be done to a body from a talented leader who everyone expects can manage problems than from a lacking leader who no one expects to seriously handle much of anything. A lacking leader may have backup ready to lend a hand when needed. A talented leader may have no backups as everyone expects that he can do any job. More talented young leaders than we may realize burn out and walk away when they see that they simply do not have enough hours in the day to solve all the unexpected problems they face. Instead of a talented young leader growing into a senior teacher and model for others, he retires early as a failure.

And woe to the Masonic body who has such a burned-out, talented leader who has bought into all the praise and ego boasting flowers thrown at him. Such a leader who develops an attitude born out of ego and pride may be worse for a lodge or body than one with no talent at all. He may listen to no one and take a very bad situation and make it impossible.

Young Masons must be on guard against taking on too much. You must know the length of your cable tow. Yes, help however and wherever you can. But do not take on so much work that you end up making a mess of everything. It is as if you were to go into a wonderful bakery with great looking and smelling treats and told that today it is all free. Know your limits. Do not gorge yourself to the point of sickness. Do not destroy your reputation and damage those who you desire to help. It is far better to truly help one than to try and help everyone only to help no one.

The Whole Truth

Winston Churchill is often quoted as saying "History is written by the Victors." On the other side of the WWII coin, Nazi propaganda chief Joseph Goebbels is quoted as saying, "If you tell a lie big enough and keep repeating it, people will eventually come to believe it." And, of course, circus owner and showman P. T. Barnum is often credited with the phrase, "There's a sucker born every minute." Put together these quotes paint a most interesting and, when we think about it, disturbing picture. What we know of the truth and what we believe to be the truth is put to the test.

But what is the truth and what is not? It may not always be as clear as we think.

There are nuances in communicating that can sometimes blur the lines between the truth and a falsehood. These "blurred lines" can be the result of unnoticed errors, lack of ability to clearly express a thought, or deliberate misdirection. The *whole truth* can be sometimes accidentally or deliberately become masked.

Failures in communicating whole truths have resulted in an often-problematic Masonic history. For example, let's look again at those above mentioned three quotes. Is there proof that the ones credited with saying these things are the authors of the quotes? No, there's not. In fact, there is serious debate as to the authorship of each of the quotes.

So, what does that mean? If someone is claimed to be the author of a quote and it turns out that he wasn't, does that mean that the quote itself should be discounted?

The three quotes are beneficial and can put us on guard against untruths. The only aspect in question are the authors of the quotes. That's the trap. The real value of these quotes stand on their own no matter who said them. But the parts in question can over-shadow the value of each quote. It's sometimes called throwing the baby out with the bathwater. When one aspect of something is discovered to be a problem, there is a tendency to throw it *all* out. What's of real value is not noticed because of the desire to be rid of what is recognized as questionable or false.

As for the quote attributed to Winston Churchill, yes, the one who wins the war makes the rules. That's been proven throughout history. To the victor goes the spoils. This is not a new concept. You have two sides with conflicting opinions or desires strong enough that they fight a war about it. If one side beats the other into submission, then *they* will be the ones who will get to tell the story of the war. Their version of the war (the history) is recorded and that's the version that will be remembered. Centuries later, all we may be able to find is that one side of the story. That one side becomes "the truth."

And then we have the Goebbels tactic which suggests that if something is repeated over and over, we often accept it *as* the truth, no matter if it is confirmed to be so or not. Showmanship and arrogant, self-assured delivery (even with no proof) does provide enough reason for some to believe whatever is said.

Does this mean that anyone who believes unconfirmed statements is a "sucker" as the quote attributed to PT Barnum implies? Well, good arguments can be made on that subject. Snake oil salesmen have always been able to make a good living. As a society, we do tend to be trusting of pleasing, entertaining rhetoric even if only seemingly of benefit to us. Proof sometimes only gets in the way of what is wanted to be believed. But there is more.

Any professional magician and many serious amateur magicians are skilled in sleight of hand. That's when your attention is drawn to one place when something important is going to take place somewhere else. It doesn't always have to be a physical distraction. It can be verbal misdirection. Sometimes a question may not be completely answered or answered in a way that points us in the wrong direction. It's not really a lie, but it doesn't lead to the whole truth.

An example of misleading by what is said would be if a friend asks you if he can borrow your car to run to the hardware store. You tell him OK, but that you need the car back soon. You ask him if he is *only* going to the hardware store. He tells you that the only thing that he needs to pick up at the store is a hammer. He says that he will be quick inside the store. You tell him OK.

Your friend goes to the store, quickly picks up the hammer, like he said, but then on the way back, stops by a friend's house and visits for a few hours. This causes you big problems, but what he told you was not *technically* a lie. Your friend did pick up just a hammer at the store, and he did so quickly. He didn't lie, but he also did not tell you the whole truth. He knew exactly what you said but misled you by leaving out a stop that he knew might give you cause to not give him what he wanted.

To understand the complete and accurate history of something or to know what someone or some people desire to do, you need to know the whole and complete truth.

So, how do we know if we are being lied to or if what is offered is not misleading? Well, we can't control what others do or say. If someone is not going to be truthful or open with us, there is little that we can do about that. But it is on us if we accept something "as fact" with no proof. If we are told things, we can and should check them out. We should not accept brand new information as fact when no proof is offered. We need to question.

If some matter is important and we receive answers that do not conclusively answer direct questions, or leaves "wiggle room," we need to pin down the one we are questioning. We do have a responsibility for what we accept as fact and truth.

If someone has a history or reputation of telling tales, then we become responsible for anything that we believe with no proof. It is our reputation that becomes at stake as well as the one telling tales. If you accept something told you from someone and it turns out to be false, there is no excuse for your accepting anything told to you by this person without proof to support what they say.

Masonic history has suffered over the years by published accounts of our history being less than accurate in many areas. For many years in the 1800s and early 1900s it was "common knowledge" that the various legends and stories of King Solomon in Freemasonry were actual historical accounts. It was not uncommon for many published accounts of history to be little more than a theory offered as a proven historical account.

We are taught very early in Masonry that we must trust our brothers. The candidate must trust the Senior Deacon for a successful degree. If the Senior Deacon does something to violate that trust, then the point of the degree is lost, and all is a waste of time and effort.

A responsible historian will write only established facts or offer new theories/information that they support with citations of where the evidence is located. A historian must not write a story based on the desires of individuals who wish to create certain outcomes.

Masons must act with honestly and integrity. We don't play games with the trust of others or listen to ideal gossip. If we are given reason to not trust another, then we must recognize that as a most serious offense. We must recognize that it is our responsibility to not disgrace ourselves or Freemasonry by either spreading falsehoods or carelessly accepting falsehoods as fact by not requiring proof before belief. Sadly, these breaches of trust have taken place and we must be on guard. We are responsible for our own actions.

Subdue My Passions
and Improve Myself in Masonry

Every new morning with which we are blessed brings both opportunities and responsibilities. Ultimately, it is up to us to either make the most out of each day or wait (sometimes for years) to regret the wasted time. In either case, the responsibility is ours to do as we judge best.

Once we step outside our doors, we enter a world of people with their own goals, ideas, and beliefs. We don't have the freedom to do *anything* that we might want to do. We become bound to the rules of the society in which we have chosen to live. If we live with others, we become accountable to them for our actions.

Freemasonry teaches us to be peaceable members of society. Freemasonry assumes that its members are not hermits but active participants in their communities. We need to interact with others to understand them. We need to learn how the group thinks and acts. Once the group's direction becomes clear, we can advance with them (if they are aligned with our way of thinking) or quit society and move on to something else. If society is not going our way, we may also decide to abandon our views to adopt the ones of society. We have choices. But what if we are unwilling to give up our own beliefs to be a part of the whole and *also* not willing to move on to something else? Right now, that seems to be the $10,000 question.

It's been a rough and mind-numbing handful of years. No matter where we are, we seem to be a divided people living on a razor's edge. Society is split and moving in multiple directions at once. No matter what we believe, many loudly disagree with us. Emotions are often raw, tempers ready to flare, and most everyone seems to be tired of worrying about so many different problems. We are seeing things happening that would have seemed unthinkable just a short time ago.

TV and social media present vastly different views designed to divide us even more. Depending on which media site we view, we are bombarded with this or that opinion. If we move to another source of information, we are bombarded with contrary views. Facts become what we are told are facts, not what is so proven. The "truth" depends on which talking head we seem to favor. We become loyal to personalities and ready to defend whatever unproven, subjective opinions that we are fed. Upset, suspicion, and discontent grow. We sometimes see our neighbors as the enemy rather than our family, struggling to survive like us. We convince ourselves that everything would be fine if only the other guy would think, believe, and act as we do. It's an impossible wish, but for too many, it's all they will accept.

And what of Freemasonry? We are part of society. We draw our members from society. It's a mistake to think we are not just as divided and divisive as everyone else. Some members are willing to speak and write extraordinarily nasty to (or about) each other. But we are *Freemasons*. We are supposed to be better than that. We are taught (or should be taught) a moral code of living. We promise to watch out and care for each other. And yet, I have personally seen things written by Masons to their brothers and posted on social media sites that would be expected from ignorant schoolyard thugs. What's happening?

Our world is changing in front of our eyes. It seems that every time we turn around, some new issue comes up that enrages us for different reasons. "I want *this* and the devil with what you want!" At some point, we must see that this attitude helps no one. But what do we do?

We can start down the road to repair by looking at the teachings of Freemasonry. We must control our own emotions. No temple can be built with divided and fighting workers. We must find the internal strength to rise above the confusion and find the peace and enlightenment that our teachings offer. No one said that being a Freemason was easy. No one said that Light comes from just waking up in the morning. It comes from hard, sincere, and dedicated work. We can find the inner peace our teachings provide. It is truly worth the effort.

When Masonic and Civil Law Collide

The Case Surrounding Etoile Polaire Lodge No. 1 vs Etoile Polaire Lodge No. 1 of New Orleans

At the opening of this paper, I should point out that I am not an attorney. It is not my goal to attempt an examination of any aspect of civil law in any state or jurisdiction. But I will offer a study of a Louisiana Masonic historical event from the 1800s. It is one that directly affects Freemasonry in Louisiana and, likely, elsewhere. In that area, I believe that I may be sufficiently qualified. Let me start with a thumbnail account of certain events from the mid-1800s.

The mid to late 1800s were a turbulent time for Louisiana Freemasonry. In 1833, the Grand Lodge of Louisiana approved a new constitution that made three different craft rituals available to lodges. The York Rite (Preston/Webb) craft ritual, the Ancient and Accepted Scottish Rite craft ritual, and the French or Modern Rite craft ritual were officially recognized by the Grand Lodge.[1] In addition, lodges worked in up to five different languages.[2] This new constitution was approved at the same time that a concordat was made between the Grand Lodge and the Grand Consistory of Louisiana. This concordat was an agreement between the two bodies that would, 1) provide for

Scottish Rite craft lodges by the Grand Lodge, and 2) Scottish Rite superior bodies would not control craft lodges.[3]

A group of English-speaking, New Orleans area Masons disapproved of the new Grand Lodge constitution and insisted that all Louisiana lodges use only the York Rite ritual and only English. These Masons felt that the lodges in the other U.S. jurisdictions worked in the York Rite and spoke English. They felt that this was reason for the Grand Lodge of Louisiana to do so. Most Masons in the Grand Lodge of Louisiana were French-speaking at that time. They felt that the multi-ritual practice of the Grand Lodge was well established and practiced in Europe. In addition, while this new constitution "officially" allowed the three rituals, Louisiana lodges had been working in these and other rituals since the early days of the Grand Lodge. The Grand Lodge also pointed out that Louisiana was established as a French territory, and New Orleans was a cosmopolitan city. The lodges working in non-English languages did so because many of their members did not speak English. The Grand Lodge felt that the demands of these English-speaking Masons were unreasonable. The English-speaking Masons felt differently.

In 1844, the Grand Lodge approved a second Constitution that reinforced the 1833 Constitution. It seemed that conflict between the groups was then unavoidable. The New Orleans English-speaking York Rite Masons felt that the 1844 Constitution of the Grand Lodge altered the Grand Lodge into a body that was no longer an Ancient York Rite Grand Lodge. This constitution was the last straw for them. In the late 1840s, these Masons created a second Grand Lodge in New Orleans.[4]

A problem faced by the Grand Lodge of Louisiana was that they realized that the Mississippi River brought a steady flow of English-speaking Masons to New Orleans — many choosing to remain. The city was growing and changing. An increasing number of new citizens from other parts of the U.S. would mean that the French would soon be in the minority. It became necessary to take this self-created Grand Lodge seriously. Fearing that the nature of the old Grand Lodge would be lost, the French sought a compromise and merger of the two Grand Lodges. That merger took place in 1850. John Gedge, who had served as Grand Master of the self-created Grand Lodge, became Grand Master of the Grand Lodge of Louisiana. Unfortunately for the French-speaking Masons, the merger turned out to be a takeover of the Grand Lodge by the English-speaking Masons. Soon after the merger, the new Grand Lodge announced that the only craft ritual that would be allowed in Louisiana was the York Rite, and the only language would be English. Lodges were told to make the necessary changes or turn in their charters. Charges of trickery abounded. Suggesting that the old Grand Lodge officers and members were upset is an understatement. Three lodges: Etoile Polaire, Los Amigos del Orden,[5] and Disciples of the Masonic Senate, turned in their charters and sought relief from the Supreme Council of Louisiana.

From its creation in 1839, the Supreme Council of Louisiana limited itself to the 4th to 33rd degrees. They did not work in or control craft lodges due to honoring the 1833 Concordat between the Grand Lodge of Louisiana and the Grand Consistory of Louisiana, at that time the highest-ranking body of Scottish Rite Masons in Louisiana. This Concordat was why the Grand Lodge, in 1833, officially acknowledged the three rituals worked by lodges under its jurisdiction. The Supreme Council of Louisiana was in "friendly and fraternal correspondence" with the Grand Lodge of Louisiana.[6] These three lodges may have given this supreme council their most significant and fundamental Masonic decision in its history.

(29)

ROYAL ARCH CHAPTERS,
Under the Jurisdiction of the Gr∴ Chap∴ of Louisiana.
CONCORD, R∴ A∴ Chap∴ No. 1, at New Orleans.
A. DERBES, H∴ P∴
PERSEVERANCE, R∴ A∴ Chapt∴ No. 2, at New Orleans.
Fr. MEILLEUR, H∴ P∴
POLAR STAR, R∴ A∴ Chapt. No. 3, at New Orleans.
R. BRUGIER, H∴ P∴
UNION, R∴ A∴ Chapt∴ No. 12, at New Orleans.
J. H. HOLLAND, H∴ P∴
DISCIPLES, R∴ A∴ Chapt∴ No. 13, at New Orleans.
L. L. VALETON, H∴ P∴

SUPREME COUNCIL
OF THE
SOVEREIGN GRAND INSPECTORS GENERAL
33d and Last Degree of the Scotch Rite.
In the United States of America, sitting in the City of New Orleans.
JAMES FOULHOUZE, Sovereign Grand Commander.
FRANCOIS VERRIER, Lieut∴ S∴ Gr∴ Comm∴ Founder.
JEAN LAMOTHE, Gr∴ Chanc∴ Sec∴ of the H∴ Empire.
J. B. FAGET, Gr∴ Treas∴ of the H∴ Empire.
J. H. HOLLAND, Gr∴ Master of Cerem∴
ROB. J. L. de PREAUX, Gr∴ Capt∴ of the Guards.
RAMON VIONNET, Gr∴ Almoner or Chaplain.
FRANCOIS MEILLEUR, Standard Bearer.
FELIX GARCIA, S∴ G∴ T∴ G∴
PIERRE SOULE, S∴ G∴ T∴ G∴
G. A. MONTMAIN, S∴ G∴ T∴ G∴

REPRESENTATIVE AND WARRANTER OF FRIENDSHIP
Of the Grand Orient of France near the Sup∴ Council.
N————.

N. B.—The Supreme Council, regularly constituted according to the Scotch Rite, is in friendly and fraternal correspondence with the Grand Lodge of the State of Louisiana, and the foreign Grand Orients; and the members of the Sup∴ Council are all officers and members in activity of the Grand Lodge.

Page 29 of the 1848 Proceedings of the Grand Lodge of the State of Louisiana

Some of the most respected Masons in Louisiana governed the Supreme Council of Louisiana. From September 20, 1845, to January 19, 1848, Past Grand Master and Criminal Court Judge Jean-François Canonge served as the Council's Sovereign Grand Commander. Upon Canonge's death in 1848, James Foulhouze, former Roman Catholic priest, and Judge of Louisiana's Second District Court, was elected Grand Commander. His Lt. Grand Commander would soon become T. Wharton Collens, Judge of Louisiana's Seventh District Court. Past Grand Masters of the Grand Lodge of Louisiana, such as John Holland, Jean Lamothe, Felix Garcia, and others, were among those serving as officers or SGIG of this supreme council. United States Senator Pierre Soulé was a respected SGIG of the Supreme Council of Louisiana. The Members were highly competent and knowledgeable Masons.

Because the Active Members of the Supreme Council of Louisiana knew the details of the 1833 Concordat between the Grand Lodge of Louisiana and the Grand Consistory of Louisiana, they knew that the three lodges had valid concerns. They knew that this Concordat had been violated by the actions of the new Grand Lodge. Because of this violation, the unyielding nature of the new Grand Lodge, and the pleas of help from the lodges, the Supreme Council of Louisiana agreed to allow the three lodges to pass under its jurisdiction. For the first time, the Supreme Council of Louisiana worked in all 33 degrees of the AASR.

By the mid-1840s, the Supreme Council, Southern Jurisdiction, USA, began awaking from its approximately 20 years of "slumber."[7] The details of what did or did not happen during the 20 or more years before they "awoke" are for another paper. For this paper, it is important to note that upon awakening, they began to see the Masonic landscape and discovered, or rediscovered, the existence of the well-organized Supreme Council of Louisiana. They also must have noticed the turmoil that was Louisiana Freemasonry. The time for the Southern Jurisdiction to act was at hand.

The Masonic "war" that had been limited to the Grand Lodge of Louisiana would soon involve the Supreme Council of Louisiana. In 1852, Albert Mackey came to New Orleans at the invitation of John Gedge to establish a Scottish Rite consistory of the 32nd degree.[8] It was a clear shot across the bow of the Supreme Council of Louisiana.

Following the 1850 merger of the two Grand Lodges and the profound discord that followed, Grand Commander James Foulhouze sought to find a way to bring peace to Louisiana Masonry. He devised a plan to include more York Rite Masons in the leadership of the Supreme Council. To do so, Foulhouze expanded the Active Members of the Supreme Council of Louisiana from nine to thirty-three. This expansion was something Albert Pike would do years later in the Southern Jurisdiction. But when challenges to the legitimacy of the Supreme Council of Louisiana began, the newer York Rite Active Members sided with the Southern Jurisdiction. Foulhouze realized that his actions were a mistake. The Council became split and divided.

Pierre Soulé resigned his seat in the Supreme Council of Louisiana due to frustration with the Council's squabbles. He was to be followed by James Foulhouze, T. Wharton Collens, and most of the officers. They stated that they could not participate in the direction the Council was taking. In

1855, a Concordat between the Supreme Council of Louisiana and the Supreme Council, Southern Jurisdiction, took place. With Foulhouze, Soulé, and other officers having resigned, the Active Members opposing the Concordat were not in great enough number to outvote the ones desirous of the merger. The vote to "merge" with the Southern Jurisdiction passed. A record of the details of how this Concordat was accomplished survives in the archives of the Valley of New Orleans. The Minutes of the Concordat state that the Supreme Council of Louisiana voted to downgrade itself into the Grand Consistory of Louisiana. The Grand Consistory would absorb the 1852 consistory created by Albert Mackey. Then the Grand Consistory would pass under the Southern Jurisdiction.

But, what about the three lodges that passed under the jurisdiction of the Supreme Council of Louisiana? They no longer had a home. With no other option, the three lodges petitioned the Grand Lodge of Louisiana to return to its jurisdiction. The petition was granted. But for two of these lodges, this move was short-lived.

About a year after the Concordat, James Foulhouze announced, without explaining how, that the Supreme Council of Louisiana continued to exist. Foulhouze reported that the ones opposing the Concordat had kept the Council alive. He said that the Council had not "slept a single instant."[9] The Supreme Council invited the three lodges to return to its jurisdiction. Etoile Polaire and Disciples of the Masonic Senate voted overwhelmingly in favor of rejoining. Los Amigos del Orden, however, stated that it grew weary of the seemingly endless fighting. The lodge desired to remain with the Grand Lodge. At this time, a most interesting series of events began. We must look at one lodge—Etoile Polaire.

Louisiana operates unlike most other states. Not only is Masonry a bit different, but most everything is different. We have parishes where others have counties. Even Louisiana's law differs from other states. The civil law is based on a version of the Napoleonic Code (yes, the French Emperor Napoleon), and this version was adopted several years before Louisiana became a state. What is accepted in courts elsewhere else may or may not be accepted in Louisiana courts. For example, in the early days of Louisiana Masonry, it was routine practice for Masonic bodies to register as state corporations. Etoile Polaire, like other Masonic lodges and bodies, was a state corporation and ultimately governed by the Civil Code of Louisiana.

Etoile Polaire's vote to pass again under the Supreme Council of Louisiana was overwhelmingly in favor of changing jurisdictions. But it was not a unanimous vote. Charles Claiborne (nephew of W.C.C. Claiborne) was elected Sovereign Grand Commander upon the resignation of James Foulhouze. Claiborne signed the Concordat of 1855. Claiborne was a member of Etoile Polaire. He was not desirous of his craft lodge passing again under the jurisdiction of a supreme council that he voted to dissolve. Claiborne and a few others voted against the move. Under Masonic law, the favorable vote was sufficient to authorize the move of the lodge from the Grand Lodge back to the Supreme Council. But this move was not just a matter of members changing jurisdictions. Etoile Polaire owned a building and property. There was a considerable amount of money at stake. Regardless of the vote, Claiborne and the

Grand Lodge objected to the move. New members were quickly added to the roles of Etoile Polaire, and the Grand Lodge took the position that the vote to move was null and of no effect. Etoile Poalire would remain on the rolls of the Grand Lodge with Claiborne and the new members. Of course, this did not stop the members who desired to pass under the jurisdiction of the Supreme Council. The result was that two Etoile Polaire Lodges (Polar Star in English) existed. One under the jurisdiction of the Grand Lodge and one under the jurisdiction of the Supreme Council. But who would get the property and money? The matter went to court.

The court case made its way to the Louisiana Supreme Court for a decision. In a nutshell, Claiborne and the Grand Lodge won the lawsuit. The lodge's property would be returned to the members who desired to remain with the Grand Lodge. But how? Why? The vast majority of Etoile Polaire's members voted to change jurisdictions. How could this not be a legal vote? The answer was that Etoile Polaire (like other Louisiana Masonic bodies) was a state corporation. A favorable vote of the vast majority was not enough. In its headnotes to its decision, the Louisiana Supreme Court wrote: "It is not within the power of the majority of the members of a corporation to dissolve it as long as a sufficient number of members to represent and continue the corporation exists." And "A resolution passed by a majority of the members of a corporation authorizing a donation of the property of the corporation to a new corporation, in which the members so voting are corporators, is unauthorized and a donation made in pursuance of it will be void."[10]

The Louisiana Supreme Court decision made it clear that the Etoile Polaire members who desired to move to the

POLAR STAR LODGE NO. 1 *v.* POLAR STAR LODGE NO. 1.

It is not within the power of the majority of the members of a corporation to dissolve it as long as a sufficient number of members to represent and continue the corporation exists.

The want of a resolution of this corporation to authorize the institution of a suit in their name can only be taken advantage of by pleading it as an exception, *in limine litis.*

A resolution passed by a majority of the members of a corporation authorizing a donation of the property of the corporation to a new corporation, in which the members so voting are corporators, is unauthorized, and a donation made in pursuance of it will be void.

APPEAL from the Third District Court of New Orleans, *Duvigneaud,* J. *J. L. Tissot, J. Q. A. Fellows* and *E. Filleul,* for plaintiff and appellant. *P. Soulé* and *C. Dufour,* for defendant.

The counsel for plaintiff argue as follows :

On the 19th February, 1855, the Grand Lodge of the State of Louisiana granted a charter of incorporation to the Polar Star Lodge No. One.

The acts of the Legislature in corporating the Grand Lodge, approved 18th March, 1816, and 11th February, 1819, provide : "That all the regular lodges, which shall be constituted by the Grand Lodge, are hereby declared to be bodies corporate and politic, in name and in deed, by whatever style or name they may be called and known in their constitution, with equal powers to those which are given to the Grand Lodge by the said act, so long as the said lodges shall remain under the power and jurisdiction of the said Grand Lodge, and in all things abide by and conform themselves to the resolutions and by-laws of the same, and no longer."

After its incorporation by the Grand Lodge, the Polar Star Lodge acquired, by an act of donation of the 3d March, 1855, the property described in the plaintiff's petition.

Louisiana Supreme Court –
Polar Star Lodge No. 1 v. Polar Star Lodge No. 1,
16 La. Ann. 53 Jan. 1861

jurisdiction of the Supreme Council of Louisiana were perfectly free to do so. But they would be creating a *new* lodge and corporation, not moving, and continuing the old corporation. So, Etoile Polaire's building, property, and bank account returned to the members of the Grand Lodge Etoile Polaire. This, logically, brings up several questions about the Concordat of 1855. This was not a 100% vote either.

Following the Concordat, the Supreme Council of Louisiana listed quite a few prominent attorneys and legal minds on their rolls. The idea that none of them realized the legal requirements for changing the nature of a state corporation, like the Supreme Council of Louisiana, is unrealistic. There is no record as to if this matter was discussed before the Concordat or if it played a part in the resignation of most of the officers before the vote. But there is also no record of any lawsuit over this change in a corporation like the Etoile Polaire lawsuit. Why?

It is impossible to get into the minds of individuals who died over 100 years ago or become a fly on the wall of meetings they may have held. But it is possible to apply logic to situations we do know. Foulhouze expanded the number of Active Members of the Supreme Council of Louisiana to accommodate York Rite members in the hopes of bringing peace to the area. That idea failed. He later viewed this action as a mistake. It is possible that Judge Foulhouze was well aware of the corporate laws of Louisiana but chose not to enforce them as it would "reset the clock." Forcing a lawsuit would have resulted in returning the Supreme Council of Louisiana to its pre-Concordat of 1855 days. Foulhouze may not have wanted the possibility of individuals that he viewed as "trouble-makers" returning to the Council. His action of making it known that the Council still survived following the Concordat suggests that he was preparing for a lawsuit if one became necessary. They also show that he was satisfied with allowing about half of the Active Members to leave, along with Supreme Council funds, if he knew that the Council would continue on the path that he and the remaining Active Members felt best.

It seems clear that the Concordat of 1855 violated the Louisiana Civil Code. Had the matter gone to court, it would have likely resulted precisely in how the Etoile Polaire lawsuit ended. The difference is that Etoile Polaire followed Masonic practices in their vote to leave the Grand Lodge. It might have violated the Civil Code, but it was proper within the laws of Freemasonry. However, the Minutes of the Concordat of 1855 shows a most unusual situation. It offers the details of a superior body downgrading itself into a subordinate body. Is that legal under Masonic law? I will decline to express an opinion on that question, but it did set the stage for some interesting Masonic "games of chess" and tactical exercises between James Foulhouze and Albert Pike. It was a most challenging time that I believe would have made the founders of Louisiana Freemasonry very disappointed. Maybe the future can be more enlightened.

Notes:

1. *Proceedings of the Grand Lodge of the State of Louisiana* (New Orleans: 1848) pp. 15-16.
2. French, English, Italian, German, and Spanish.
3. *Proceedings of the Grand Lodge of the State of Louisiana* (New Orleans: 1848) p. 16.
4. Michael R. Poll, "The Elimination of the French Influence in Louisiana Masonry," The Scottish Rite Papers, (New Orleans, LA: Cornerstone Book Publishers, 2020), 29-39.
5. Los Amigos del Orden and Silencio lodges merged in 1880 to create today's Cervantes No. 5.
6. *Proceedings of the Grand Lodge of the State of Louisiana* (New Orleans: 1848) p. 29.
7. Charles S. Lobingier, *The Supreme Council, 33°* (Louisville, KY: The Standard Printing Co., Inc., 1931), 151.
8. James Foulhouze, *Historical Inquiry* (New Orleans: Cornerstone Book Publishers, 2011 reprint of 1859 edition) 62-63.
9. James Foulhouze, *The Masonic Delta* November 1857 (New Orleans, LA)

10. Louisiana Supreme Court, 16 La. Ann. 53 (1861), Polar Star Lodge No. 1 v. Polar Star Lodge No. 1 (https://cite.case.law/la-ann/16/53/)

Bibliography

- Charles Laffon de Ladébat, translator & notes, *A Masonic Trial in New Orleans.* (New Orleans, LA: J. Lamarre, 1858).
- Charles S. Lobingier, *The Supreme Council, 33°* (Louisville, KY: The Standard Printing Co., Inc., 1931).
- Ray Baker Harris, James D. Carter *History of the Supreme Council, 33° Southern Jurisdiction, USA (1801-1861)* Washington, D.C.: The Supreme Council, 33° 1964).
- Michael R. Poll, "James Foulhouze: Sovereign Grand Commander of the Supreme Council of Louisiana," *Heredom*, vol. 6, (Washington, DC: The Scottish Rite Research Society, 1997) pp. 49-82.
- Michael R. Poll, "The Early Years of the Grand Consistory of Louisiana (1811-1815)," *Heredom*, vol. 8, (Washington, DC: The Scottish Rite Research Society, 1999-2000) pp. 39-54.
- Michael R. Poll, "Albert Pike's Address before the Grand Consistory of Louisiana," *Heredom*, vol. 10, (Washington, DC: The Scottish Rite Research Society, 2002) pp. 223-242.
- Charles Laffon de Ladébat, *The Schism between the Scotch & York Rites* (New Orleans: Cornerstone Book Publishers, 2008 reprint of 1853 edition).
- James B. Scot, (Author) Alain Bernheim, (Foreword), Michael R. Poll, (Afterword), *Outline to the Rise and Progress of Freemasonry in Louisiana* (New Orleans, LA: Cornerstone Book Publishers, 2008 reprint of 1873 edition).
- Robert B. Folger, *The Ancient and Accepted Scottish Rite in Thirty-three Degrees* (New Orleans, Cornerstone Book Publishers, 2011 reprint of 1862 edition).
- James Foulhouze, *Historical Inquiry into the Origin of the Ancient and Accepted Scottish Rite* (New Orleans, LA: Cornerstone Book Publishers, 2012 reprint of 1859 edition.).
- Arturo de Hoyos & S. Brent Morris, (Editors), *Cerneauism and American Freemasonry: Essays by Alain Bernheim, Arturo de Hoyos, S. Brent Morris, and Michael R. Poll* (Washington, DC: The Scottish Rite Research Society, 2019).
- Michael R. Poll, *The Scottish Rite Papers*, (New Orleans, LA: Cornerstone Book Publishers, 2020).

The Mystery of Mysticus

Time is a questionable commodity. It can drag on or pass in the blink of an eye. It all depends on our actions and feelings toward any task. It's been over forty years since I joined the Scottish Rite, and my feelings toward its philosophy have hardly changed an iota. The time has truly seemed to pass in that single blink of an eye. Time is nothing when studying the Scottish Rite's philosophy. I am as amazed and fascinated with the teachings of the Rite today as I was when I was first exposed to this metaphysical gem. That's right; I said "metaphysical." Some seeking only the outer layers cringe at such terms when describing the Scottish Rite. They may also view gumbo as only another soup.

Early in my Masonic life, my interest in the deeper, metaphysical aspects of the Rite led me to study the people and history of this system. It was there that I hit a snag. I could find so few original documents on the early history of the Scottish Rite. Sure, I could find books on its general history, but when dealing with the mid-1800s, they all told very different stories depending on the author and jurisdiction. In many of the old historical accounts, there was a great deal of open hostility, mean-spirited attacks, and … emotion. I wanted to find original documents to sort the evidence out and reach my own conclusions. But these were the pre-internet days. To conduct research, I had to travel to where the documents resided. That was easier said than done.

I made several trips to the House of the Temple in the late 1980s and early 1990s. Before these trips were numerous communications via letter with Ill. John Boettjer, 33°, then the Editor of the *New Age* (and the renamed *Scottish Rite Journal*); Ill. Dick Matthews, 33°, Grand Archivist; Ill. Bill Fox, Sr., 33°, Grand Historian; and Mrs. Inga Baum, Librarian. All were extremely helpful and supportive in my searches.

Some months following these trips to the House of the Temple, I was conducting one of my favorite pastimes — visiting used bookstores in New Orleans. In such shops, I could find rare, long out of print books that might assist me in my Scottish Rite research or serve as a source of enlightenment. In one shop, I stumbled on a gold mine of a find. It was three huge boxes filled with near-mint condition copies of the *New Age* from 1907 till the late 1970s. The shop was selling the entire lot for $40.00! I quickly paid the man (fearing he might realize the paltry sum he was asking) and loaded the boxes into my car.

For the next few weeks, I savored my literary haul. The dated artwork and even old advertisements of pianos and shotguns drew constant smiles from me. Different periods reflected various themes in the *New Age*. The WWII years were filled with patriotic pieces. However, the period around 1915-1920 displayed a most interesting tone in the publication. The papers were unquestionably metaphysical. All manner of metaphysical subjects were explored in the various issues. Authors even took to identifying themselves under exotic pennames. One such author identified himself as *Mysticus*. His articles began showing up in numerous issues. Every paper that he contributed was thought-provoking and written to engage the reader. But who was this author?

I was intrigued. In the June 1920 issue of the *New Age*, a column was written by *Mysticus* titled "A Corner of the Library." In this column was a piece he called, "Collectors of Occult and Magical Books" (p 271). *Mysticus* wrote:

"Washington City is a well-known center of scientific and philosophical inquiry. Some twenty-one years ago, there existed in the capital a little band of independent thinkers of which I was a member. We were students of philosophy, folklore, symbolism, occultism, and psychic research. We called ourselves, jokingly, "Dwellers on the Threshold," a title borrowed from Bulwer-Lytton's strange Rosicrucian story, "Zanoni."

Well, just that paragraph alone interested me to no end. Who *was* this *Mysticus*? What was this group? The article mentions several Illustrious Brothers and even Harry Houdini as members. I would have loved to have been a fly on the wall of one of their meetings. *Mysticus* continued:

"The leader of this group was Dr. [Leroy M.] Taylor, a man of wealth and a prodigious collector of occult literature. We met at his house every Saturday evening to discuss problems in philosophy and religion, particularly those bordering on the mystical, for which the doctor had a decided penchant."

And also,

"The collection of Dr. Taylor, which is now in possession of the Supreme Council and is elegantly displayed in the House of the Temple, is a library of the occult sciences."

In my early visits to the House of the Temple, I remember seeing parts of the Taylor Collection. I believe it has now been broken up and is no longer an intact display.

Mysticus also wrote:

"One morning, I received a note from Dr. Taylor asking me to come to his house and examine a magic mirror which he had purchased. Anything in the magic line was certain to enlist my interest."

Mysticus continued and explained that several friends experimented with this "magic mirror," but they neither had success with it nor experienced any supernatural events. He then goes on to say that another Mason decided to experiment with this mirror. That Mason was Ill. Thomas H. Caswell, 33°, Sovereign Grand Commander of the Supreme Council, SJUSA. *Mysticus* wrote:

"At last, a strange incident happened, which is best described by John Elfreth Watkins, in a communications, at the time, to the *New York Herald*, July 30, 1899.

"Some interesting experiments are now being made with a "magic mirror" lately purchased by Dr. L. M. Taylor, of Washington. To the history of the instrument are attached many weird traditions. It was found in India by a woman greatly interested in Oriental occultism, and after her death was sold to its present owner.

"This mirror has generally been employed merely as a means of entertainment. Many men have played with it without serious anticipations. It was in this spirit that Thomas H. Caswell, Sovereign Grand Commander of the Scottish Rite of Freemasonry, sought solitary seances. While he sat, earnestly gazing into the magic mirror, suddenly the reflected shadows seemed to focus themselves into a vivid picture. The Sovereign Grand Commander distinctly saw an illuminated casket containing the body of a man.

"Gazing steadily, he saw the features brought more clearly into focus and suddenly recognized the body as that of a prominent member of the Scottish Rite order in the South. Mr. Caswell was surprised, but not alarmed. He confided the experience to several friends, but made light of it. He had not heard from his friend in the south for some time. He was entirely ignorant as to the state of the latter's health, yet a few days later this same friend died and his death was announced to Mr. Caswell. Several prominent men testified that the name of the deceased had been confided to them by the Sovereign Grand Commander before the death occurred. Neither Mr. Caswell nor any of the witnesses is an occultist or a spiritualist in any sense of the word."

The early 1900s were a true metaphysical Renaissance in the United States. Many groups existed to study just about every aspect of the metaphysical and occult sciences. While this account with Ill. Caswell is certainly intriguing and mystifying; I wanted to be focused on my original question. Who was this *Mysticus*? He had to be a prominent Mason in the Scottish Rite's inner circles. But what was his name? I decided to write to Dr. Boettjer with that question. Ill. Boettjer wrote back saying that he could find no information on this *Mysticus* and passed the question to Mrs. Baum. Soon, I receive a letter from Mrs. Baum with the same conclusion. She had no success in her searches and said she was enlisting Ill. Bros. Fox and Matthews in the hunt for evidence. However, the outcome was the same. There was no information that anyone could find on the identity of *Mysticus*. I was disappointed.

Believing that I had reached a dead-end in the search for the identity of *Mysticus,* I decided to put the project on the shelf and move on. I went back to those old copies of the *New Age* to randomly explore them for other interesting bits of information. Then I happened upon something written by *Mysticus* that made me sit up straight in my chair. This was in the December 1916 issue of the *New Age* and again in his column, "A Corner of the Library." This segment was titled "The Works of General Albert Pike" (p 562). *Mysticus* wrote the following of Pike:

> "I often saw Gen. Pike on the streets of Washington, DC. His snow-white hair falling about his shoulders like the mane of a lion ..."

I knew that sentence. I had seen it (or something close to it) somewhere before. But where? After thinking about it, I pulled out my copy of Manly P. Hall's 1960, *The Phoenix,* published by his Philosophical Research Society. On page 38, under the chapter, "Albert Pike, the Plato of Free-masonry," was the same (but not exact) quote. The quote was possibly rewritten or edited, but it seemed too close to be written by someone other than *Mysticus*. However, Hall did not mention

Henry R Evans, 33°

Mysticus. He credited the quote to "Henry R. Evans, Inspector General, Honorary, of the Supreme Council, 33°." Bingo! I had not seen that anywhere before! It was much easier to gather information on Henry R. Evans. To my great surprise, he was the *Editor* of the *New Age*! In addition, the clear love of magic shown by *Mysticus* was also shared by Evans. I sent all this information to Mrs. Baum. Before long, I received a large envelope in the mail. It included a good deal of information on Evans, including his admission that he was *Mysticus* in a letter to Ray Baker Harris. Of course, to this day, I don't know how Manly P. Hall knew that Henry R. Evans was *Mysticus*. Maybe they met, communicated with each other, or who knows? This is a perfect subject for new research.

Just as the philosophy of the Scottish Rite can have layers, so can this mystery involving Henry R. Evans / *Mysticus*. There is possibly more as to why Evans wrote these metaphysical pieces, why he wrote under a pseudonym, and why time seems to have made such writings almost nonsensical to many Masons today. We must do the work to

Feby 23/48

R. Baker Harris, 33°,
  Librarian,
    House of the Temple,
      1733 16th St., N.W.,
        Washington, D.C.

Dear Bro. Harris :
            Your letter of Feby 17 is received.
I am honored to know that you have a folder in
your reference file, containing copies of my articles
contributed to The New Age Magazine. Of course you
know that everything appearing under the nom de plume
of Mysticus was written by me; but you are not
aware (I imagine) that I also used another nom de
plume — "Magus," for 4 contributions. The editorials
written for The New Age were never signed. I wrote
many of them. I send you herewith a list of the
more important ones; also references to the "Magus"
material.
        Fraternally yours,
          Henry R. Evans, 33°

Personal letter from Henry R. Evans, 33° to Ray Baker Harris, 33°.

discover the reasons. Time can be our friend or our enemy. It doesn't care. We are made up of things we have done only if we can remember what we have done. This is why history, and its proper recording are essential. If over time, we forget things that may be important to the whole story of us, then we (as well as our philosophy — who we are at our heart) may, over time, change. We may forget who we are. It is subjective if that is good or bad, but it's not accurate. Dr. Henry R. Evans — *Mysticus* — influenced many Masons with his words. He was an enlightened man. We owe him and ourselves to know, understand, and remember him.

Clarifying Masonic History

I'm looking at a hardback copy of Albert Mackey's classic two-volume *Encyclopedia of Freemasonry*. It is the 1929 edition revised by Robert L. Clegg. Page 774 of the second volume says that Albert Pike was "Born at Boston, Massachusetts, December 29, 1809." On page 604 of that same volume, under the "Louisiana" section, it states, "On June 19, 1813, Charters were granted to Albert Pike Lodge of Perfection, No. 1, and Eagle Council of Kadosh, No. 6, at New Orleans." If each quote is read independently of the other, we find two bits of information to which a reader may or may not pay much attention. Either quote might be cited by someone writing a paper dealing with the material. If, however, they are read together, well …. hmmm. The quotes say that New Orleans Masons in 1813 chartered a Lodge of Perfection in the name of a three and a half year-old Albert Pike! Well, that's not what happened. It's just a mistake — a typo in the book. If you pay close enough attention, you will rarely find an error-free Masonic book (no matter how talented, dedicated, or well-known the author). We are human, and mistakes do happen. When these gremlins pop up, we correct them and move on. But errors, even significant ones, are not this message's point.

Responsibility in communications is the point of this message. It is often said that our Masonic history is a mess or is far from completely understood. Well, that's true. But who is responsible for accurate accounts of history? I remember a discussion I had with a Mason some years back. He retold a bit of Masonic history that his mentor had provided him years before. It was verifiably incorrect. I pointed out the error and offered to show him where he could find the correct information. I failed to consider that this Mason held his mentor on a pedestal and was not only emotionally loyal to him but very ready to defend any perceived "attack" on his name. He became offended at my suggestion that his mentor had made an error. He told me in an indignant manner that what he said *was* correct because "Brother […] told me that it was correct, and he was *never* wrong!" He offered no evidence to support his claim but held firmly to his opinion because … well because he *wanted* to believe it. So, how do we deal with errors in Masonic history which are believed because some *choose* to accept the mistakes written or spoken by their Masonic heroes?

I believe that there is a shared responsibility in what we believe of any communications. Today, the standard for writers of Masonic history is, "You write it or say it; *you* prove it." A Masonic historian who writes papers without effort to support new information is considered a hack. Such practices will result in a horrible reputation. But still, things that are written and published carry weight. Some will believe anything offered (even with no support) if it is provided by someone they consider "important." I have seen booklets written by persuasive Past Grand Masters from the early 1900s, saying, "The first Grand Master in Freemasonry was King Solomon." I doubt that any thinking Mason today would accept such a statement as accurate, but years back, many Masons did. Readers of Masonic history should not believe things written just because they are written. Both share a responsibility.

If accurate Masonic history does not matter, if facts don't matter, then Masonry means nothing. We can't stop honest errors or even ones that are less than innocent. But conscientious writers will do what is needed to establish the accuracy of what they have written before sharing it with others. They will correct errors when discovered.

On the other hand, we must take responsibility for what we accept as gospel. If we read unverified bits of information and then pass on what we have read with no attempt to determine its accuracy, then we are no more than spreaders of idle (and maybe dangerously incorrect) gossip. Facts do matter. Freemasons purport to be Seekers of Light — of truth. It is hardly enlightened to pass on unproven claims under the guise of "facts." It does not matter the source. Light is not shades of gray.

When Did Operative Masonry Turn into Speculative Masonry?

I was contacted by a young Mason with a question about the early history of Speculative Freemasonry. He said that he had initially believed that modern Speculative Masonry evolved out of the old Operative Freemasons, but then he read something that discounted that idea. He wanted to know my thoughts on the matter.

OK, let's talk about it. To start with, this will mostly be an opinion paper based on what I feel is a logical examination of available information of the early days of Speculative Freemasonry. We have many missing or non-existent records, and so much is left to the best guess of whoever is writing the history. In addition, the history of Operative Freemasonry is even more lacking. Yes, we know some things, but so much is anyone's guess.

When you take these situations and couple them with the very valid demand of "you say or write it, you prove it," then it makes for a very problematic situation. Any quick answer can bring discredit to the one saying it. To understand this situation, we need to understand what Operative Freemasonry means, what Speculative Freemasonry means, and what "evolving from" means. Or, at least, we need to agree on some common understanding.

First, what was a lodge of Operative Freemasons? Well, it can be looked at as a union of sorts. Skilled workers in the building trade or guilds could find employment through membership in such lodges. Someone would want something built, and they would contract an Operative lodge to build it. The lodge would provide all the workers needed. All the workers would be required to be able to travel to wherever the work site was located. This is what is understood as a "free-mason."

One who was a member of an Operative lodge could not be a bondsman, slave, or indentured servant. They needed to be able to travel to wherever the jobs would take them. Another thing about an Operative lodge of Freemasons is that they did not have only stonemasons as members. The buildings built by these lodges also needed carpenters and workers in metal, glass, and other artisans. It was a worker's union of all those who participated in the construction of a building.

We can also find evidence that Operative Lodges were also training schools where young men who desired to one day join the lodge as full members (and workers on building projects) could learn as apprentices. So, an Operative lodge would be a place to learn and obtain work.

Now, if we look at almost any Masonic history book, we will find an English minor aristocrat and alchemist named Elias Ashmole. On October 16th, 1646, he was said to have written in his diary that he joined Warrington Lodge. So, what was Warrington Lodge? What does his joining this lodge mean? And is the diary entry accurate?

From available records, Warrington Lodge was an Operative Lodge of Freemasons. It seems that Ashmole joined an Operative Lodge but had no interest in becoming an Operative Freemason. He had other reasons for becoming a member. The suggestion is that this is early evidence of a Speculative Freemason.

As to if Ashmole's diary account is accurate, well, I have not seen any lodge record of him — maybe there is one, but all that I have seen are reported entries from his diary. The best that I can do is look at the situation from a logical standpoint. I can examine what I know and don't know and give an opinion based on what I believe is probable.

Let's step back for a moment and look at what was happening around that time. If Warrington Lodge was a lodge of Operative Freemasons, it would have been a place of employment for workers in the building trade. Why would they have an interest in someone joining them who was *not* a skilled craftsman?

If what we know about the history of the great European cathedrals is accurate, then the largest and greatest ones were built between the general time of 1000 and 1500 AD. By the time Ashmole is reported to have joined, the building trade seems to have gone into a decline. Operative lodges may have needed help finding work for their craftsmen. But again, why would a lodge of Operative Freemasons have any interest in someone who was *not* a skilled craftsman joining them? How could his joining an

Operative lodge be of any benefit to anyone? For that matter, what would it be about a trade guild that would be of any interest to someone like Ashmole?

We need to step outside the known information and standard reports to take another look at the situation from both sides. We also need to realize that we can't look at past events using our knowledge of events today. The truth is that the common lodge experience in the US today is dramatically different than the typical US lodge experience from the early to mid-1800s or even 1900s. We must realize that we are wholly unfamiliar with the lodge experience of an Operative lodge in England in the 1600s or earlier.

If we were somehow transported back in time to the initiation of Elias Ashmole, we would undoubtedly be in a very different world. But, even with the clear understanding that the lodge experience of Ashmole was very different from the lodge experience of Masons today, more is needed to answer the *why* of the question. Why would either the lodge or Ashmole have any interest in this initiation taking place?

Let's look at the lodge first.

If this was a lodge of Operative Freemasons and it had been experiencing a good number of years of declining work, it would likely be in some financial trouble. The lodge would need income to pay the bills as well as the workers. If someone like Ashmole was willing to pay to be "accepted" into the Operative lodge, then why not take his money? If any work came, he would *not* be sent out with the other workers. He was not an actual Free Mason. He was an "Accepted Mason."

When we look at the situation in this light, it is reasonable for such lodges to create a special category for individuals of good character willing to pay the lodge for something akin to honorary memberships. This type of special category would make sense for the lodge, but it does not explain why individuals like Ashmole would have any interest in such a lodge.

From what we know about Elias Ashmole, he was a very accomplished individual. He was an alchemist, an astrologer, a solicitor (English attorney), a founding Fellow of the Royal Society of London, and a collector of many rare manuscripts. He showed interest in basically all the seven liberal arts and sciences.

Ashmole was a most interesting and talented man of metaphysical, spiritual, and scientific thought. So, why would he even entertain the idea of joining such a guild? Well, maybe because this was not just some collection of hard-working laborers.

The Freemasons had always possessed a unique reputation in all the areas where they visited and worked. Most people spent their lives in the small communities where they lived. They would work until nightfall and then come home. This was their life and was repeated each day until they died. It was a big deal when travelers from out of their area came to town.

By the mere fact of their traveling from area to area, the Freemasons grew in knowledge. They became educated in many subjects by exposure to them in their travels. In the evenings, stories were shared from areas they had never seen (and likely would never see). They developed a mystique.

By the 1500s, the Dark Ages were ending, and what would follow was the Reformation and then the Age of Enlightenment. Individuals like Ashmole were some of the early leading figures in this new desire to learn, explore, and grow as humans. With all the subjects that interested Ashmole, the mystique of the Freemasons and their "secrets" must have called to him.

Ashmole was hungry for knowledge and wanted to learn firsthand the Freemasons' secrets. He reached an agreement with them and was accepted by a lodge. Interestingly enough, after joining, his diary shows him rarely participating in the lodge. There may be good reasons for his lack of participation.

We must remember that an Operative lodge of Freemasons was *primarily* a worker's union. They existed first and foremost to find work for their members. Ashmole could very likely have found the business meetings of the lodges very dull. But that's only a guess based on the man's reported interests and the fact that after joining, he rarely attended.

If the lodge had been active in the areas where Ashmole held great interest, he might have attended far more often. Again, these lodges, regardless of their reputations, were primarily worker's unions designed to train and find building jobs for their workers. These workers wanted to put food on their tables and went to the lodges to find jobs. They had a very different reason for going than Ashmole.

Over the next 100 to 150 years, the building trade declined even further. We also find traces of Speculative Lodges of Freemasons during this period. These would be made up solely of those who did not consider themselves Operative Freemasons or construction workers.

When we step back, it does seem a most interesting time. Operatives Masons went to the lodge to find work to put food on the table. The Speculatives went to lodge to discuss more esoteric subjects alluded to by the Operatives and maybe expand on them.

For one, the lodge was a practical experience designed to find work, for the other, it was an educational experience designed for personal enlightenment. With such different goals, it seems odd that they would have been mixing at all.

In 1717, the Grand Lodge of England was created to organize lodges of Speculative Freemasons. Speculative Freemasonry took off and spread all over the world like dry houses on fire. To say that it became popular everywhere it was organized is an understatement.

Operative lodges certainly did not benefit from the wildfire, worldwide growth of Speculative Freemasonry. It was apples and oranges. The Speculative lodges offered what was widely sought by the common man — education and enlightenment.

But, as time passed and interest continued to grow, members wanted to know more of the history of Speculative Freemasonry. Unfortunately, here is where problems began. Claims of Freemasonry going back to the days of King

Solomon were not uncommon. Glorified, royal histories seem to be desired. These wild claims have damaged serious Masonic research and caused some to doubt the ability of Masonic organizations to conduct objective research into its own history. Too much of what was presented as history was fantasy.

Let's try to bring this all together and look at it. The old Operatives made their living by working in the building trade. Speculative Masons make their living from all jobs under the Sun. The old Operatives met in lodges to train, learn about, and find jobs in the building trade. Speculative Masons met in lodges to discuss theories, ideas, and lessons designed to improve themselves.

Yes, we can find records of some who joined Operative lodges and did not seek involvement in the building trade. Yes, Operative Freemasonry was declining when Speculative Freemasonry was on the rise. Yes, Speculative Freemasonry was created on the perceived model of Operative Masonry. The working tools, jewels, stations, and ranks were tweaked, used, and assigned various moral lessons.

It is not possible to look at Speculative Freemasonry without considering what we know of Operative Masonry. The two are intertwined by centuries of real, imagined, or borrowed association. Speculative Freemasonry is, at the very least, heavily inspired by the model of the old Operatives. That seems clear. But to say that Operative Freemasonry transformed itself into Speculative Freemasonry is something that I don't personally believe can be proven.

Individuals who were inspired by the lore of the old Operatives likely created something based on them and gave it the touches they believed suited their needs and wants. It is possible that some who may have joined Operative lodges with no intention of working in the trade felt that this gave them certain rights to create their own Masonic lodges, even if they were a bit different than the ones they joined.

Anyway, that's my take on the matter. I don't see that we can prove much more than what is already out there without new information being discovered — which is always possible. Of course, in the end, I don't think it matters. The lessons of Speculative Freemasonry are valid and have stood the test of time.

Speculative Masonry does not have to be thousands of years old to be valid. If Masonry is, at all, declining today, it is not because of the lessons taught by our lodges. The problems may be coming from the *lack* of those lessons being taught.

The Dangerous Mason

Recently I was scanning random videos on the internet. I came upon a police public service video on self-defense. At the very beginning, the officer made a point of saying that if anyone is ever held up, they should remember that nothing they have is worth more than their life. They should comply with whatever the robber demands. This public service video reminded me of the Hiramic Legend and his situation in this story. I've talked about this in several other papers, but I'd like today to take it in a different direction.

Hiram valued his integrity over his own life. It is a powerful and meaningful lesson. But, in thinking about it, how realistic is it today? I have never heard of anyone today threatening someone's life over the secrets of Freemasonry. But we could look at this lesson of integrity a bit differently and use something that some may experience as an example.

Recently, I received a phone call from a brother. It had been a while since we had spoken. During our conversation, he mentioned that a certain Masonic "leader" had threatened him. He said that he might be denied this or that if he did not do certain things that this individual wanted him to do.

109

The brother told me that he told this leader that he was not looking for anything in Masonry and only sought to learn the lessons and apply them to his living a better life. He said that if he were denied anything by his refusal to accommodate him, it would only mean that he would have more time to spend with his family. This "leader" told him that if this was the case, then he was a very dangerous Mason. Let's think about this.

Why would this Mason be "dangerous"? All he said was that he put doing the real work of Freemasonry ahead of just making other Masons happy. Well, saying only that means that he cannot be controlled. Leaders with limited ability (but amble ego and hunger for power) depend on quality Masons doing their bidding and making them look good.

But, more than that, a disobedient, quality Mason might encroach on his little kingdom and take power away from him. That is certainly a reason for such a "leader" to view someone as dangerous. It is certainly a reason for such an individual to follow through with threats to deny the Mason this or that award, office, or honor.

We can see this as a non-violent situation as Hiram faced. The "bad guy" wants something. He threatens to get it, and if he does not receive what he wants, he punishes the Mason who refuses to accommodate him. It's a very similar and alarming situation.

We have had a lack of any real Masonic education, coupled with declining memberships, for so many years now that many lodges and other bodies are truly hurting for members. Sometimes the leaders are chosen based only on whoever is there on election night. In too many bodies, a qualification for leadership is simply the ability to show up at meetings.

It's great if someone knows Masonry, but some bodies are so dysfunctional that being there is more important. So, when a young Mason with ability shows up at meetings, he is grabbed by all. Everyone wants him. He may end up burning out and walking away from everything or ends up doing a poor job due to being overworked. Many truly care about Masonry and feel that it will hurt Freemasonry itself if they don't do all they are asked.

We face challenging times ahead. We all know that. Many lodges need help, but most hard workers are stretched to their limits. We do what we can, but we must properly balance our time. Integrity means doing something to help Masonry, not spinning our wheels. It is also not doing something with the goal of getting rewards. We must walk away from those who would threaten us into doing their bidding. We must look inward and know if we are doing things to help or only to gain something from one known to be a "big shot."

Our goal in Masonry is self-improvement. We are to learn and pass on what we have learned. Anything else puts us on a perilous path. Integrity guides us to look inside and know why we are doing things, and if true Masonry is the goal. If you are dangerous because you are trying to improve yourself, help where you can, and know what real honors are, then dangerous is a good thing to be. We need more such dangerous Masons.

Why is Everyone Looking at Me?

A common problem faced by more than a few new lodge officers is feelings ranging from nervousness to visible panic when presiding in the East. The same is true of delivering lectures, or any sort of speaking in public. I well remember my own fear when I first sat in the East. It felt as if every member of the lodge was staring right at me just waiting for me to make a mistake. It wasn't true. They were thinking nothing of the sort, but it was sure how it felt.

If you feel uncomfortable (to any degree) with public speaking or presiding over any lodge or body, you are far from alone. Studies show that upwards of 75% of the population have some level of fear when speaking before any gathering.[1] The level of destress can range from feelings of mild discomfort to open terror. The underlying concern would seem to be anxiety of negative judgment or evaluation by others. We want others to think well of us and putting ourselves "out there" for examination or review can cause severe reactions in some. But why?

Regardless of the level of our intelligence, much of what humans do is instinctual — automatic. We don't think about when or if we need to breath or blink, we just do it. Fear is also something that often comes on us with no advance thought. We may be walking down the street and then turn into a dark alley. The sudden darkness and sight of the alley might well generate some level of fear in us (or, at the very least, heightened awareness). It's logical. Something or someone might be in the shadows ready to jump out and harm us. We don't think, "Well, it's time now to become alarmed!" It just happens. Some feelings or actions of the body occur without any obviously command from the brain. Our mind does seem to operate to a great extent on its own. We may memorize a phone number, but we "know" some things in the deepest parts of us that were never learned by us. That's instinct. Certain events or situations set off unconscious responses from our emotions or body.

Self-preservation is deeply engrained in us, and fear is the warning signal that something may harm us. This is all clear and obvious. But how does this apply to something seemingly so innocent as public speaking or sitting up in the East of a lodge? Let's go back in time and look for clues.

Early humans gathered in groups or tribes as a means of self-protection. They knew they were safer in a group than on their own. It was a dangerous, deadly world. Being thrown out from their group would certainly be a death sentence. As such, they did not want to displease the group or do anything that might cause the group to expel them. We can even look at the fact that expulsion is the greatest actual punishment in Freemasonry. In the Medieval days, to be expelled from an Operative Masonic lodge would mean that the Mason could no longer feed or provide for himself or his family. It was still a very harsh time, and an expelled Operative Mason would be in a serious situation. Displeasing the group has always been something that we wanted to avoid. It brings on something akin to fear in us deep down in our hidden recesses.

I don't intend to go into any sort of deep psychological examination of the human psyche, but we should be aware of some things that affect us in daily life. Being judged harshly by others can trigger that "Oh, oh" switch in us. At the very least, most of us don't like it when someone openly expresses displeasure with us or something we did. Being in front of a group of our peers and speaking, or running the operation of lodge, can flip that switch. Even if we have no reason at all to believe that anyone has any reason to criticize us, we may experience anxiety before speaking before a group. And what if we were criticized? What could anything that anyone says justify the actual panic that some feel before public speaking? It is not logical when we think of our lives today. But humans are extraordinarily complex and carry deep unconscious memories from our earliest existence.

Let's look at a few things that can be done that may make presiding and public speaking a bit easier. Let's first look at sitting up in the East.

The first time that you sit up in the East can be a daunting experience. Looking at the lodge room from anywhere else in the room is very different than looking at it from the East. From the perspective of the East, you realize that all eyes are looking up at you. They look to you for guidance and leadership. What you give them often depends on your level of preparedness for sitting in the East.

First and foremost, know your work. There is no debate. If you accept the office, you need to make the time to learn and do the work. Only the unworthy "title seekers" accept officers with no plan of doing the work necessary for the success of the body. The ritual may seem to be a hurdle you need to overcome, but it can truly be a safety net for you. Knowing exactly what you need to do and say will afford you *far* more confidence in your station. Rehearse again and again and again. Do so alone or with others who can help you. It's always wise to have someone who is proficient in the ritual sitting near you in lodge. No matter how well anyone knows his lines, anyone can, at any time, go completely blank. A quick, soft prompt from one close to you is far better than the look of silent, hopeless terror on the face of a Worshipful Master who has gone blank followed by half a dozen loud prompts from the sidelines (with some loud prompts being completely wrong).

Organization and planning are also vital for a successful Worshipful Master. You should know all that will come to your desk at meetings. Plan the order and try to know ahead of time anything out of the ordinary. Knowing exactly what you have in front of you will remove much of the pressure of the office. Stay in constant contact with your secretary and officers. With your focus on what you are doing next, you will many times almost forget that there is a group of Masons out there looking at you.

Engage with the lodge members at the start of each meeting. As soon as the lodge is open, tell them, "Good evening, my brothers!" Every time I've heard this said in a lodge, the response is extremely positive and friendly. The return greetings should alleviate any concern about how the lodge truly feels about the Master. It will put you at ease. It is not a matter of "them over there" and "me over here." It becomes us.

Another matter that is not discussed enough is attempts at reading the faces of those on the sidelines. In short, don't do it. Humans do not have the ability of reading minds and when facial expressions are used to determine what someone is thinking or feeling, complete mistakes most often follow. A Worshipful Master who tries to gage the feelings or thoughts of the lodge members by expressions on their faces opens himself to a great deal of unnecessary misunderstandings.

To highlight the matter of miscommunications when trying to read faces, I was once in a lodge listening to various discussions from the sidelines. It was an uneventful meeting. After the meeting was over, the Worshipful Master rushed down towards me and took hold of both of my arms. In a worried tone he asked, "Are you okay? Did Bro. "XYZ" do or say something to upset you?" I had no idea in the world what he was talking about. I said that the brother did nothing at all and pointed out that he was sitting across from me on the other side of the lodge. The Master told me that he was worried because all evening he saw me looking "upset" and staring with an "angry look" at Bro. "XYZ." I again was confused as I was unaware of looking at anyone with any such look. I certainly had no issues with the brother in question. To prove my point, I took the Master with me over to Bro. "XYZ" and told him what the Master told me. The Brother was as confused as me. He told the Master that apart from friendly greetings when I came into the lodge, he had no other contact with me, certainly nothing of any sort of a disagreement. The Master walked off as confused as the two of us.

Later that evening, I thought of something that happened the day before. My wife and I had gone to the grocery and picked out a package of chicken that we planned for dinner. When my wife began preparing it, she was shocked at the bad smell of the chicken when she opened it. She then saw on the wrapper that the "sell by" date had passed a few days before. Neither of us had noticed it when we bought it. We were not very happy. We ended up having takeout pizza that night. The point is that I remember thinking about the "chicken event" at the lodge meeting. It is very possible that I did have an unhappy look on my face thinking about that bad chicken. Since I was sitting across from Bro. "XYZ," it is possible that the Master thought that I was looking at him and that he had somehow upset me. This example is why it is risky to make assumptions of how others think or feel. If I had happened to have been looking at the Master rather than across the room, he might well have come up to me asking why I was upset with him. It would have been just as incorrect.

When presiding in a lodge or any Masonic body, a good idea is to find two or three chairs and spots in the room where no one is sitting. When speaking to the lodge, move your eyes back and forth to these locations. The members won't know that you are focusing on empty chairs and will think nothing of it. You won't be seeing faces and having those "inner gremlins" making you think completely incorrect things. Before each meeting have a serious talk with yourself. Just because someone has an unhappy expression on their face does not mean that they are upset with you or anyone else. If someone laughs, it does not mean that they think you are a joke. The lodge members will look to the East because that is the center of the lodge activity, but they are sitting there many times in their own personal thoughts having nothing at all to do with you or anyone else in the lodge. They are unaware of anyone looking at them or trying to understand what they are feeling. They are mostly just in their own thoughts.

And then we have cases when someone is delivering a lecture. That brings more issues.

Just as sitting in the East, when you deliver a lecture there is no excuse for not knowing your lecture inside and out. Do not believe that you can simply "do it off the cuff." That kind of thinking opens you up for a world of problems. Plan your talk, organize it in a clear & understandable manner, and stick to the plan. Practice, rehearse, practice, rehearse. Make that your mantra.

Just like when in the East, don't be misled by trying to read faces or expressions. Don't fall into the trap of thinking that others are trying to judge or grade your performance. The vast majority are just there to listen to what you have to say with no prejudgment.

In delivering a lecture to a lodge, start off with the same sort of greeting that you would as a presiding officer. Let the audience know that you appreciate being before them and thank them. But be careful with telling jokes at the start to "lighten up" the audience. Telling jokes is like singing. Some people have beautiful singing voices, and some could not hit the right notes or keys with a shotgun. Singing is a talent that some have, and others simply do not have. The same is true of telling jokes. Unless you have been making others laugh with jokes since childhood, avoid doing something that could start off your lecture with the awkward silence that follows a badly told joke.

Make yourself realize that you are not delivering a lecture to be evaluated by the audience. You are there to help them better understand what you are going to teach them. Turn your focus to enlightening the ones in front of you. A successful lecture should mean that you have helped bring Light to the ones listening to you. Focus your concentration on the subject of your lecture and on helping the audience. Recognize that you are the teacher. Don't focus on trying to please the audience. Know that they want what you have. Your job is to give it to them.

Another problem for some speakers is when they take a very good lecture subject and turn it into a very difficult listening chore for the audience. It is when someone reads their lecture from printed pages. Having written notes or subject points to keep you on track is great and highly advised, but to read the lecture can sometimes turn on you. Reading in a manner to engage the audience is a skill/talent that not everyone possesses. As in singing or telling jokes, what the audience hears coming from your mouth is appreciated only when certain requirements are met (and this in no way deals with the lecture content requirements). Someone reading in a monotone voice will bore listeners regardless of the quality of the paper. Humans respond to rhythmic voices with inflections and proper pauses for emphasis on important aspects of what we are saying. In conversations with others, we use inflections, pauses, and even tone or volume changes in our speech. We do this naturally, without thought. But when we read from a page, we often use one single tone and speed (except for stumbles over mispronounced words). Those who believe that they have nothing to worry about (or need not prepare for a lecture because they have it printed out) are often in for unexpected, unpleasant surprises. The bottom line is that unless you are trained in reading from a prompter or printed page before others, try to avoid it. It can create a very poor performance.

There are a few cases and situations where reading from a printed lecture is required. If this must be done by you, then there is even more need of practicing your lecture. Read it again and again until it becomes almost memorized by you. Read it enough times that you become familiar with the natural inflections and rhythms of the words — practice, rehearse, practice, rehearse. There is no way around it.

The anxiety of speaking before others (from the East or delivering a lecture) can be overcome by you. It requires understand of why you feel this way and doing the things necessary to overcome these feelings. The human mind is a powerful tool. It can get away from you or can be used by you to help in ways you may not always imagine.

Notes:

1. (https://www.psycom.net/glossophobia-fear-of-public-speaking)

Acting Masonic

Over the years, the most common email I receive concerns how young Masons are deeply disappointed that Freemasonry in practice acts like any other minute's reading, dues collecting club. Many walk away and never look back. But, in other cases, how they are treated in a lodge, Grand Lodge, or other bodies is the cause of the problems. Let's look at this.

One young brother told me that he spoke with his Grand Secretary about something having to do with their Grand Lodge session. He was the Junior Warden of his lodge. He said he had never met the Grand Secretary before and asked him a few questions. He said the Grand Secretary spoke to him like he was ignorant, worthless, and unworthy of even speaking with him.

I've known many Grand Secretaries over the years who are as friendly, helpful, and welcoming as can be, but it only takes one bad apple to sour a young Mason forever. I have seen some who receive this or that position, and ego drives them to believe that they are all important. They act as if you don't have titles, degrees, or honors behind your name, then you are no one. For some, that belief is used as a control tool. "Do what I tell you, or you will be denied this or that."

In another case, I was told of an event where a Mason who I knew spoke to a young Mason in about the same disrespectful and unMasonic manner. I was having difficulty believing this account as I knew this Mason. He was always friendly and helpful to me, and I saw him being helpful and friendly with others. It turns out that the account was true, but his attitude was due to his having a horribly bad day. This example leads to the point of this paper.

Very few would argue that it has been a difficult few years. We are only now beginning to see the final pages of a horrible pandemic that has crippled the world. You will rarely meet someone who does not personally know someone who has died or has been extremely ill from COVID.

Gas and food prices are going through the roof, the economy is horrible, and we are a politically divided and unyielding nation. On top of that, we seem to be having mass shootings at schools, churches, public shopping places, and everywhere nearly every time we turn around. We all seem to be living on an emotional roller coaster, with no idea what may come next. I believe we need to rethink some things.

Pressure is and has been building in everyone. Yea, there are times when someone speaks and acts like a jerk because that's what they are. But sometimes pressure causes very good people to break and explode. First impressions are only sometimes accurate.

Yes, we must realize that not all in Masonic positions of authority belong there, and some may not even belong in Masonry. We have for too many years placed almost no guards on the West Gate, and we are paying the price for it. But our problems involve more than just the unworthy.

The times we live create stress because of everything around us and the events we are exposed to daily. Most everyone has snapped and blown up in ways that may not have happened at different times. We must acknowledge that the times we live are unique and require taking more than a beat or two when passing judgment on our brothers.

In his classic movie, "The Great Dictator," Charlie Chaplin said in his extraordinary speech, "more than cleverness, we need kindness and gentleness. Without these qualities, life will be violent, and all will be lost."

No matter what we think or believe, we have choices in life. We may have no choice in events around us, but we have total choice over our actions. We can control how we think and act. But just as these are facts, it is also a fact that we can easily slip and act in ways that do not represent who we are inside.

As Freemasons, we are expected to be peaceable members of society and act with honor. We understand that no one is perfect, but we are to continually work to be better and watch out for our brothers. There is a responsibility that we all have regarding conduct. We need to control our own emotions and passions. We must be aware of how we act and speak. We need to respect ourselves and others.

We also need to realize that sometimes we fail and fall under pressure. We need to realize that of us and others. If we fail to be and act how we should, we need to make amends. If we see others who fall to the pressures of situations, we must understand that we all fight silent battles within us.

We must not make snap, unyielding judgments as to the worthiness of others. We must be generous in forgiving others and not judge harshly for offenses made due to situations faced by us all. The fall others make today may be made by us tomorrow.

More of what we are doing needs to be fixed. There is too much anger, nastiness, and fighting in the world. Too many only point fingers at the other guys and see themselves as the complete victims. No one ever said that following Freemasonry's teachings would be easy. We should never be quick to anger or when responding to acts that may be the result of internal battles.

It's a hard time for us all. Let's try some understanding when we speak, act, and respond. Help each other. Support each other. Be kind.

Glimpses into Another Masonic World

A Look at the 1812 and 1818 Proceedings of the Grand Lodge of Louisiana with Commentary

While visiting a bookstore, I happened upon a book filled with black & white photographs of downtown New Orleans from the 1950s and 60s. The manner of dress, the cars, the stores, and the general feel of the times were clear in these photos. I was born in the fifties and remember many of the stores and the area's look. So very much has changed since that time. So many memories came back.

When we look at photos from the past, we can gain ideas of how people lived "back then." It was not only their manner of dress and the "old look" of stores that were different. Even buildings we know are a bit odd in old photos — familiar but not really the same. When looking at the past, we need to remember that daily life was not the daily life of today. Buying things from stores was a different experience. Communicating was different. Travel was different "back then," as was almost everything in their day-to-day life. They were humans just like us, but their lives were filled with events foreign to us in the "modern world." It was a different life experience in the 1950s. It was different in the early 1900s and very different in the early 1800s. Each generation saw

127

innovations in daily life that made their same 24 hours unlike people before them. Freemasonry is the same.

We are kidding ourselves if we believe today's lodge experience is like the lodge experience of the 1950s. And certainly, today's lodge is vastly different from the 1850s or earlier times. But what was it like going to lodge in times long before we were alive? Without good Minutes and records, we can only guess. The lodge Minutes give us an idea of the lodge's activities. The more care and details included in the Minutes, the more future generations will know and have available to understand the lodge and what transpired.

And then there is the Grand Lodge. One of the best ways to look at the history of any Grand Lodge is to look at its Proceedings. The Proceedings are the published accounts of the Grand Lodge's activity. Like a lodge, the more detail in the Proceedings, the better chance we have of understanding the events, decisions, and nature of the Grand Lodge and the lodges under its jurisdiction for that year.

A problem with early Louisiana Masonry is that several decades of significant early Proceedings do not exist. I don't mean that they were never written or published; I mean they were somehow destroyed either by accident or deliberately. We have no record of what happened to them. Most of the very early years are missing up until 1818, and then the very controversial and troubled years of the mid to late 1830s and early 1840s. We can only guess what happened during those years.

It was a most difficult time in the mid-1800s for Louisiana Masonry. Passions ran high, and "the other guy" was viewed as the "problem" of everything. Some may have believed that various aspects of Louisiana Masonry were better lost than preserved. Too much of our Masonic history was lost because a few believed a recreated past of their liking was better than the actual history. It is truly a sad situation.

The task now falls on objective historians of today to try and piece together those critical missing years, but not with any political desire for specific outcomes. The research must be done with the sole desire for the facts. It must be void of Masonic political considerations or desires. Step by step, with sincere objectivity being the rule and guide of the researchers, we can rediscover those early years.

I'd like to now take a look at the time of the creation of the Grand Lodge of Louisiana, along with several very interesting documents in need of examination. I believe that this time is a very rich source of valuable research for any objective, sincere Masonic researcher. There is so much that still needs discovery.

Let's start this journey with the Extracts of the 1812 Proceedings of the Grand Lodge of Louisiana. This is a record of the events just before and after creating, the Grand Lodge of Louisiana.

EXTRACTS from the Records of the GRAND
LODGE OF LOUISIANA, Ancient York-Masons.

(Sitting of the 16th of May, 1812.)

WHEREAS, at a Grand Communication of Ancient
York-Masons, held in the City of New-Orleans, State
of Louisiana, at the Lodge room of the Worshipful
Lodge *La Parfaite Union*, No. 29, situated in the
Suburb St. Mary, corner of Camp and Gravier streets,
on the 15th day of May, in the year of our Lord 1812,
and of Masonry 5812.

" It was unanimously *resolved* " that the Worship-
„ ful Master of the W. Lodge *La Parfaite Union*,
„ No. 29, the Senior of the Regular Lodges of this
„ State, be requested to issue his Summons to the
„ Masters, Past-Masters and Officers of the several
„ ancient and regularly constituted Lodges in this State,
„ to meet in Convention, to take into consideration the
„ interests of the true Craft, and to deliberate on the
„ necessity of establishing a GRAND LODGE in this
„ State ".

(Sitting of the 13th of June, 1812.)

Whereas, at a Grand Convention of Ancient York-
Masons, held in the City of New-Orleans, State of
Louisiana, in the Lodge room of the W. Lodge *La
Parfaite Union*, No. 29, situated in the Suburb St.
Mary, corner of Camp and Gravier Streets, on saturday,
the 13th of June, in the year of our Lord 1812, and of
Masonry 5812.

PRESENTS

First, The Worshipful Master, Past-Masters and
Officers of the Worshipful Lodge *La Parfaite Union*,
No. 29, regularly constituted by the Right Worshipful
GRAND LODGE of South Carolina, by Warrant bearing
date the 21th of November, 1793.

To the left is the first page from the Extracts of the 1812 Proceedings of the Grand Lodge of Louisiana. The first entry is for a meeting reportedly held on May 16, 1812. But there appears to be a typo on the meeting date. It states in the first line (in parenthesis): "Sitting of the 16th of May, 1812." But, in the first paragraph, it then states that this meeting was on the "15th of May." I don't know which is the correct date.

Regardless of the actual date of the meeting, it was held at Perfect Union Lodge for the purpose of discussing and authorizing a Summons to be sent out to "the several ancient and regularly constituted Lodges in this state." The goal of the Summons was to gather these lodges to meet and "to take into consideration the interests of the true Craft, and to deliberate on the necessity of establishing a Grand Lodge in this state."

There are several things in this first page that I find interesting. Regardless of if the meeting was held on the 15th or 16th of May, it was held only several weeks after Louisiana became a state on April 30, 1812. It seems that these Masons wanted to waste no time in establishing a Grand Lodge. The second is how they identified the lodges who were to receive this Summons. Note how Perfect Union is identified as the "Senior of the *Regular* Lodges of this State." I'll talk a bit later about their interesting use of the phrase "Regular Lodges."

The page goes on to speak of a convention held at Perfect Union on June 13th, 1812. Five lodges attended this convention. Perfect Union No. 29 is the first lodge listed. They were constituted by the Grand Lodge of South Carolina on November 21st, 1793.

(2)

2d. The Worshipful Master, Past-Masters & Officers of the Worshipful Lodge *La Charité*, No. 93, regularly constituted by the Right Worshipful GRAND LODGE of Pennsylvania, by Warrant bearing date the 1st of March, 1802.

3d. The Worshipful Master, Past-Masters & Officers of the Worshipful Lodge *La Concorde*, No. 117, regularly constituted by the Right Worshipful GRAND LODGE of Pennsylvania, by Warrant bearing date the 29th of October, 1810.

4th. The Worshipful Master, Past-Masters & Officers of the Worshipful Lodge *La Persévérance*, No. 118, regularly constituted by the Right Worshipful GRAND LODGE of Pennsylvania, by Warrant bearing date the 27th of October, 1810.

5th. The Worshipful Master, Past-Masters, & Officers of the Worshipful Lodge *L'Etoile Polaire*, No. 129, regularly constituted by the Right Worshipful GRAND LODGE of Pennsylvania, by Warrant bearing date the 3d of June, 1811.

The Grand Convention having met agreeably to Summons issued by the W. Brother P. F. DUBOURG, present Master of the W. Lodge *La Parfaite Union*, No. 29, for the express purpose to take into consideration the interests of the true Craft, and to determine whether it wou'd be advantageous to establish a Grand Lodge in the State of Louisiana.

The following motion was made and seconded, viz : That saturday next, the 20th of June, be the day appointed for the election of the Grand Master, the Deputy Grand Master and other Grand Officers, to form a Grand Lodge for the State of Louisiana, free and independent of all other Masonick Jurisdiction, under the style and title of Grand Lodge of Louisiana, ancient York-Masons. The said motion was, *Nemine contradicente*, agreed to.

Page two continues with the list of lodges attending the June 13th Convention. Charity Lodge No. 93 is the second lodge listed. They were "regularly constituted" by the Grand Lodge of Pennsylvania by a warrant dated March 1st, 1802.

The third lodge is Concorde No. 117, also constituted by the Grand Lodge of Pennsylvania on Oct. 27th, 1810.

The fourth lodge is Perseverance lodge No. 118, again constituted by the Grand Lodge of Pennsylvania on Oct. 27, 1810. The same day as Concorde Lodge.

And finally, Etoile Polaire No. 129 was constituted by the Grand Lodge of Pennsylvania on June 3rd, 1811.

This listing of lodges, along with their dates of constitution, reflect the numbering when the original Grand Lodge of Louisiana charters were given to the founding lodges. The Lodges were Perfect Union No. 1, Charity No. 2, Concorde No. 3, Perseverance No. 4, and Etoile Polaire No. 5.

Three of the five founding lodges still exist and only two maintain their original numbers, Perfect Union No. 1, and Perseverance No. 4. Etoile Polaire today carries the No. 1 as does Perfect Union—why will come later in this paper.

Page two continues with an explanation that this convention was called to discuss if the lodges felt it would be "advantageous" to create a Grand Lodge in Louisiana. They apparently felt it was as they agreed to meet again on June 20th to elect Grand Officers. The name that they agreed to give to this new Grand Lodge was "Grand Lodge of Louisiana, ancient York-Masons."

(3)

(Sitting of the 20th June, 1812.)

And Whereas, at a Grand Convention of Ancient York-Masons, held on the 20th June 1812, and of Masonry 5812, at the Lodge room of the Worshipful Lodge *La Parfaite Union,* No. 29, situated as above, being the day appointed for the election of a Grand Master, Deputy Grand Master and other Grand Officers, to form a Grand Lodge for the State of Louisiana, free and independent from all other masonick jurisdiction, under the Title and Denomination of GRAND LODGE OF LOUISIANA, Ancient York-Masons.

The Convention proceeded by ballot to the election of the aforesaid Grand Officers, and on casting up the votes, it appeared that the Right Worshipful Brethren, herein after named, obtained a majority, and were duly elected to the dignities of the Grand Lodge, to wit :

The Worshipful P. F. DUBOURG, present Master of the Worshipful Lodge *La parfaite-Union,* No. 29, GRAND MASTER.

The Honorable and Worshipful L. C. MOREAU LISLET, Past-Master, & Member of the Worshipful Lodge *L'Etoile Polaire,* No. 129, DEPUTY GRAND MASTER.

The Worshipful Jean BLANQUE, present Master of the Worshipful Lodge *La Charité,* No. 93, SENIOR GRAND WARDEN.

The Worshipful François PERNOT, present Master of the Worshipful Lodge *La Concorde,* No. 117, JUNIOR GRAND WARDEN.

The Worshipful J. B. PINTA, present Master of the Worshipful Lodge *La Persévérance,* No. 118, GRAND TREASURER.

J. B. VERON, present Senior Warden of the W. Lodge *la Persévérance,* n° 118, GRAND SECRETARY.

Page three reports on the Convention held on June 20th, 1812. Most Louisiana Masons recognize that as the date of the creation of the Grand Lodge of Louisiana. The meeting was held in the lodge room of Perfect Union No. 29.

The reports states that they began the process of creating the Grand Lodge by the election of Grand Officers. The first five Grand Officers elected came from the five lodges that formed the Grand Lodge. But the order in which they were elected is interesting.

The Founding Grand Master was P. F. Dubourg, the sitting Worshipful Master of Perfect Union No. 29.

The Deputy Grand Master was L. C. Moreau Lislet. He was a Past Master of Etoile Polaire No. 129.

The Senior Grand Warden was Jean Blanque, the sitting Worshipful Master of Charity No. 93.

The Junior Grand Warden was Francois Pernot, the sitting Worshipful Master of Concorde No. 117.

The Grand Treasurer was J. B. Pinta, the sitting Worshipful Master of Perseverance No. 118.

The Grand Secretary was J. B. Veron, the Senior Warden of Perseverance No. 118.

(4)

The Worshipful Mathurin PACAUD, Past-Master and Member of the Worshipful Lodge *L'Etoile Polaire,* No. 129, GRAND ORATOR.

YvesLEMONNIER, present Junior Warden of the W. Lodge *La Charité,* No. 93, GRAND PURSUIVANT.

Augustin MACARTY, present Junior Warden of the W. Lodge *La Parfaite Union,* No. 29, GRAND STEWARD.

In the same sitting, the Right Worshipful GRAND MASTER was duly & regularly installed, proclaimed, saluted and congratulated, agreeably to ancient form and usage.

It was moreover unanimously *resolved* by the Grand Convention, that the R. W. Grand Master should be authorised to install the other Grand Officers elected, and to designate a convenient day for their installation, and the opening of the Grand Lodge.

(Sitting of the 11th *July,* 1812.

And Whereas, saturday, the 11th day of July, in the year of our Lord 1812, and of Masonry 5812, having been fixed upon by the R. W. Grand Master for the Installation of the Grand Officers, and for the opening of the Grand Lodge.

The Members of the Grand Lodge of Louisiana, met agreably to the Summons, to them directed by the R. W. Grand Master, in New-Orleans, at the Lodge room of the Worshipful Lodge *La Parfaite Union,* situated as aforesaid, and the R. W. Grand Master proceeded to the Installation of the Grand Officers elected, according to the order of their respective dignities, and the said Grand Officers were duly proclaimed, saluted and congratulated agreably to ancient form and usage, which proceedings appear more fully on the Records of the Grand Convention and of the Grand Lodge.

Attest

Deron

Grand Secretary

Page four begins with the appointment of the Grand Orator, Grand Pursuivant, and Grand Steward. The date of July 11th, 1812, was set for the Grand Officers' installation and the Grand Lodge's opening.

The closing section is for the July 11th sitting of the Grand Lodge. Perfect Union was again the location of this meeting of the Grand Lodge. The RW Grand Master installed the Grand Officers, and all the Grand Officers were duly proclaimed, saluted, and congratulated agreeably to ancient form. The document closes with the signature of the Grand Secretary.

Now, obviously, this small document does not present a complete window into the events surrounding the creation of the Grand Lodge of Louisiana. We know only what was recorded, some of which may be far from crystal clear.

We can only guess at the conversations held about the creation of the Grand Lodge of Louisiana by the various Masons. There are no records (of which I am aware) of conversations held over dinners, lunch meetings, or several Masons having coffee on a French Quarter balcony. Logic tells us that these sorts of meetings must have happened. But what was discussed? What was the tone? Were they friendly meetings, strictly business, or could some of the discussions have become heated? We can't be sure. But there are clues that we can examine.

In several places, we see mention of "regular lodges." Perfect Union was identified as the "senior of the regular lodges" in Louisiana. Yes, if this new Grand Lodge desired to join the US Masonic community of Grand Lodges, they would need to show that the lodges were regular. But really, their regularity would already be established by the fact that they all held warrants or charters from well-recognized and regular Grand Lodges.

So, why did the new Grand Lodge members need to qualify their lodges as "the regular ones"? There seemed to be a desire to separate themselves from lodges in the state that may *not* be considered regular. But which lodges and why were they not considered regular? There were not many lodges in the area at that time.

Two English-speaking lodges in the New Orleans area withdrew from the convention to create the Grand Lodge. But they belonged to the very well-recognized Grand Lodge of New York. They would only be considered regular. The only other lodge I know of at that time was le Bennifiance lodge. This lodge was created in 1807 by three 33rds under the jurisdiction of the Supreme Council at Kingston, Jamaica. It was the first actual Scottish Rite craft lodge created in New Orleans. Could this be the lodge that was considered irregular? If so, why? The same 33rds who created this lodge in 1807 created a Scottish Rite Lodge of Perfection in 1809 and a Grand Consistory in 1811. Most all the early Grand Lodge officers belonged to this Grand Consistory.

Why would the members of the Grand Lodge consider one body as regular and the other (from the very same source and being of the same nature) irregular? It does not make sense. To understand the situation and certain words and phrases used, we may need to carefully read some of what was written into this report. Let's take Etoile Polaire lodge as an example.

According to this report, Etoile Polaire received its charter from the Grand Lodge of Pennsylvania on June 3rd, 1811. When the Grand Lodge was created, the numbers given to the founding lodges appear to be given out by seniority, with Perfect Union being the senior or oldest and given the No. 1. Charter numbers 2, 3, & 4 were given to the lodges with charter dates of 1802 and then two lodges in 1810. Etoile Polaire, with its 1811 charter date from Pennsylvania, appears to be the junior of the lodges and given the No. 5. But, while all of this is true, it is not the whole truth and can be very misleading.

Etoile Polaire was not the junior lodge by its creation date. Etoile Polaire was organized in 1794. Only Perfect Union has an older creation date of 1793. So, why was Etoile Polaire not given the No. 2 slot? Why was its charter from the Grand Orient of France ignored? At that time, the Grand Orient was among the world's most respected and regular GLs.

Also, why did Etoile Polaire move from the Grand Orient to the Grand Lodge of Pennsylvania? And most of all, why was the second oldest lodge made to seem as if it was the junior of the five lodges creating the Grand Lodge? Nothing is recorded in this excerpt to explain this, but we can read a bit between the lines.

At the time of the creation of the Grand Lodge of Louisiana, the Grand Orient of France was a very well-recognized and regular Grand Lodge. In fact, recognition *from* the Grand Orient was highly desired. So, why did Etoile Polaire move from the Grand Orient to the Grand Lodge of Pennsylvania about a year before the creation of the Grand Lodge of Louisiana?

To understand the actions of the early New Orleans Masons at the time of the creation of the Grand Lodge, we may need to step outside of Freemasonry. We need to look at the city and the culture of the individuals.

Louisiana became a state in 1812, but it had gone through a tough 50 years before achieving statehood. The people were *different* and often difficult to understand for those living outside New Orleans. It was not just that they mainly spoke French, but there was just something about them. Something that most outsiders just couldn't put their finger on, but it was something. And the French of New Orleans knew this about themselves. Something about being a part of the United States appealed to the French in New Orleans. They wanted to do all in their power to show that this was what they wanted, even if they still needed to fully understand the consequences.

I don't want to get into a complicated history of Louisiana, so we can simply say that the area was discovered in 1682 when La Salle landed on the Mississippi Gulf Coast and claimed all the area for France. Here is a thumbnail account.

New Orleans was founded in 1718 by Bienville. In its early days, New Orleans was not exactly a hot spot for visitors, and there was no line of prospective settlers signing up for this new city. After all, the area was a marsh overrun with snakes, alligators, and bugs of every kind. In addition, it was hot, humid, and flooded every year. Any wonder why people were not exactly lining up to relocate?

France was in both a good and bad position. They knew they had an excellent location as they could see how a port right at the mouth of the Mississippi River leading into the Gulf of Mexico would be a significant money maker for them. But how could they develop this port if no one was interested in living in the city? Well, the French government came up with a fascinating and creative solution to their problem.

The French government decided to go to the Bastille and make an offer to a good number of prisoners. They would set them free if they would relocate to New Orleans, agree to live there and, of course, never return to France. Not surprisingly, they quickly found many takers for their offer. But this only solved half of the problem.

A city filled with only men would not last that long. They needed women as well. So, to solve this problem, they went to several of the brothels around Paris, arrested a good number of the *workers,* and made them the same offer — Bastille or New Orleans. Again, New Orleans was the winner. So, with this interesting collection of original citizens, New Orleans was off and running.

In not too many years, the French government was able to attract more respectable transplants. The city started to grow and develop its own personality. Masons visited the city, and in 1752, the first lodge arrived in New Orleans. Within just a few years, several lodges and bodies of high-degree French-style Masonry were created. Then the bottom dropped out.

Between 1756 and 1763, France and England fought what became known as *The Seven Years' War*, also known as *The French and Indian War*. When it became clear that France was about to lose the war, it realized that England would take possession of its land in the New World, including the Louisiana Territory and the valuable port of New Orleans.

So, in a secret agreement, France gave Spain ownership of the Louisiana Territory with the understanding that, at some point, the territory would revert to France. During the time that Spain owned the area, it would keep all the profits generated. That was a good deal for Spain and France but not so good a deal for the citizens of New Orleans.

The citizens of New Orleans knew little to nothing about this deal with Spain, and then suddenly, Spanish soldiers and government officials arrived in New Orleans. The residents of New Orleans felt betrayed by France. They had felt like second-class citizens for a long time, and this only validated these feelings.

The Spanish brought a totally different culture and way of living. The residents of New Orleans did not like it. From a Masonic standpoint, this was terrible news as the Spanish outlawed Freemasonry.

A revolt took place and was quickly, and harshly, put down by the Spanish. The Worshipful Master of the oldest lodge in New Orleans was killed by Spanish soldiers when they came to his home to arrest him. Other Masons were arrested and sent to prisons in Cuba. Freemasonry disappeared from the area. At least, that's what we believe.

Records of New Orleans Freemasonry have yet to be discovered from the late 1760s to the creation of Perfect Union in 1793. But if (and it is a very speculative "if") these 1750 & 60s lodges went underground, could they possibly have existed around the time of the creation of the Grand Lodge and were viewed as "irregular"? Were these the "irregular lodges" from which the founding lodges wanted to distance themselves? There is no evidence one way or the other.

But, if the "lost lodges" were gone and no longer existed, then why did the lodges at the time of the GL creation feel the need to qualify themselves as "the regular lodges" if no other lodges of any kind existed?

By the time the Grand Lodge of Louisiana was created, nearly 100 years had passed since the founding of New Orleans. The citizens of New Orleans were no longer former prisoners or prostitutes. They had developed a complex culture and social structure. But no matter how cultured, wealthy, or evolved the French of New Orleans had grown, a part of them still viewed themselves as unwanted French stepchildren.

They were bitter that the French had abandoned them to the Spanish. Their culture was French in nature, but it began to change. They maintained the French language but began identifying themselves as Creoles far more than French.

Regardless of their initial dislike of the Spanish, they began to embrace some of that culture and even architecture. Close ties developed between New Orleans and places like Cuba and Mexico. Then Spain returned Louisiana to France.

Before they had even decided whether this was good, France sold Louisiana to the United States. Now, *that* was interesting to the Creoles of New Orleans.

The truth was that the New Orleans Creoles were very different in nature and culture from the Americans — more so than even they realized, but the Creoles found great respect in the American fight for freedom. It appealed to them, and they saw their becoming Americans as positive.

The "American Dream" appealed to the New Orleans Creoles, and I believe the most remarkable example of their desire to be an actual part of the United States came just a few years after the creation of the Grand Lodge and during the Battle of New Orleans.

Louisiana played no real part in any aspect of the American Revolution, but the Creoles viewed the 1815 Battle of New Orleans as a chance to prove themselves as part of the American effort for freedom. When Andrew Jackson came to the city to begin its defense, the Creole Militia made themselves available to Jackson. Jackson reviewed this militia and was frankly less than impressed.

The Creoles had dressed in their finest uniforms with bright colors, shiny medals, and large plumed hats. Jackson was later reported saying that this militia looked more suitable for marching in a parade than fighting a battle.

Jackson relegated the militia to the French Quarter for its defense. But when reports reached the city that the main battle had begun at the Rodriguez Canal some five or six miles below the city, the Creoles were horrified. They were *not* going to be denied their chance to fight in this battle.

So, with full packs and rifles, the New Orleans Creole Militia went to the levee alongside the Mississippi River and ran at full speed the entire distance to join in the fighting. They did prove themselves.

If we take this powerful desire of the people to be a part of the United States and apply it to Freemasonry, we may see a different view of "regularity."

If we look only at the 1812 excerpts concerning Etoile Polaire Lodge, then, with no other information, we might assume that Etoile Polaire was created in 1811. Its charter from the Grand Lodge of Pennsylvania says 1811. The fact that it was created in 1794 and previously held a charter from the Grand Orient of France is nowhere to be seen.

So, why did Etoile Polaire turn in their charter from the Grand Orient of France for a new one from Pennsylvania? Why were they moved from the number two slot to the number five slot giving the appearance that they were a brand-new lodge, the junior lodge out of the five? I believe it was due to the strong desire to be a part of the United States.

Suppose the early Louisiana Masons viewed regularity as it is commonly viewed by Grand Lodges today. In that case, nothing makes sense about the creation of the Grand Lodge of Louisiana. However, if we take the idea that Grand Lodges in the US needed to be created by lodges holding charters from other US Grand Lodges, things start to fall into place. Even if this is not the actual policy, it does seem to be how early Louisiana viewed regularity.

They seem to have felt the need for all the lodges that would create the Grand Lodge of Louisiana to hold charters from US Grand Lodges. Le Bennifiance did not seem to desire a US charter, and they were left out. Etoile Polaire only requested a US charter just about a year before the creation of the Grand Lodge. It is possible that they were threatened with being left out if they did not make this move.

It seems that lodge regularity was viewed at that time and at least partly as holding a charter from a US Grand Lodge. And then this would be used by a new Grand Lodge to gain admittance to the US family of Grand Lodges.

I truly would have loved to have been a fly on the wall during the discussion when the officers of Etoile Polaire were told that they would be given the junior and No. 5 slot in the creation of the Grand Lodge. I cannot imagine that the meeting went very well. But that was the way that it went.

I believe the compromise reached was that while they would receive the No. 5 slot, the first election of officers would give Etoile Polaire the first Deputy Grand Master.

I also believe this situation played a large part in Etoile Polaire's 1833 drive to obtain the first Scottish Rite charter. And when that charter was revoked by the new Grand Lodge in 1850, Etoile Polaire demanded to keep the No. 1 slot resulting in there being two lodges today listed as No. 1 — Perfect Union and Etoile Polaire.

New Orleans Creoles have never taken well to insults, and long remember them. They always seem to find some way to make such insults costly.

Of course, this paper only addresses some of what possibly happened during the creation of the Grand Lodge of Louisiana. Much is yet to be discovered. But it is certain that with every door that is opened, two new doors will be discovered in need of opening. If the desire to learn and discover remains, I know we will uncover more of our past and learn more of who we are.

Now, let's look at the next surviving Proceeding, the 1818 Proceedings of the Grand Lodge of Louisiana.

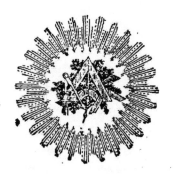

GRAND LODGE

OF THE

Most Ancient and Honorable Fraternity

OF

Free and Accepted Masons

OF THE

STATE OF LOUISIANA.

At a quarterly Communication held in the City of New-Orleans, on Saturday the 26th. day of December, Anno Lucis 5818, in ample forme, were present,

THE BRETHREN

Lewis Moreau-Lislet, *Grand-Master,*

J. B. Modeste Lefebvre, *Deputy Grand-Master,*

J. B. Desbois, *R.·. W.·. Senior Grand Warden,*

Yves Le Monier, *R.·. W.·. Junior Grand Warden,*

Augustus Guibert, *R.·. W.·. Grand Secretary,*

J. B. Pinta, *R.·. W.·. Grand Treasurer,*

The page to the left is the first page of the oldest known and complete Proceedings of the Grand Lodge of Louisiana. These Proceedings cover the transition from Lewis Moreau-Lislet as Grand Master in 1818 to J. B. Modeste Lefebvre as Grand Master in 1819.

The Proceedings, being only six pages, are not exactly filled to the brim with details. But we can still learn a good deal of interesting information from what is offered. For example, these quarterly Communications held by the Grand Lodge were held the day after Christmas. I find that very interesting and dedicated. It is also interesting that while it says that the meeting was held in New Orleans, the exact location is not provided.

The 333 St. Charles Ave. location, where several Masonic Temples were built, was not used until 1853. Before that time, the Grand Lodge must have met in one of the area lodges. The only clue most often given in the early Proceedings is that the Grand Lodge met at the "hall of their sittings." That's not exactly specific.

Looking through the pre-1850 Proceedings, we can pick up only a few clues. We can see that the first meeting of the Grand Lodge, the meeting creating the Grand Lodge, was held in Perfect Union Lodge. At that time, Perfect Union met at the corner of Camp and Gravier Streets. They would later move to Rampart Street, a few blocks from the existing site of Etoile Polaire. But can we understand "hall of their sittings" to mean Perfect Union? Not really.

Page 9 of the 1828 Proceedings tells us, "The Grand Lodge met in the hall of Polar Star Lodge (its usual place of sitting) at the hour of half past 11 o'clock AM and was opened by the Grand Master in ample form." So, was Etoile Polaire the "hall of their sittings"? Well, from page 3 of the 1845 Proceedings, "The Grand Lodge holds its meetings in New Orleans at Perseverance Lodge No. 4 corner of St. Claude and St. Ann streets."

It would seem that until the Grand Lodge had its own building, it rotated between the several New Orleans area lodges. They may have had some internal method for selecting which lodge hall would be used for the Grand Lodge meetings, but it is not clear in the Proceedings.

Another thing that needs to be stated, but becomes apparent on page three, is that this Dec. 26th Communication was for the Installation of the Grand Lodge Officers. They were elected at a previous Communication in November and installed at this Communication. Reading this first page by itself, however, can lead the reader to assume that the election was held on Dec. 26th

[2]

William S. Hubert, *R.·. W.·. Grand Orator,*
John Pinard, *R.·. W.·. Grand Tyler,*
Stephen Berthel, *Grand Poursuivant,*
Augustin Macarty, *Grand Marshal ;*

And all the others Grand Officers, Ex-Grand Officers, and Members of the Grand Lodge and the representatives of the Lodges under the jurisdiction of the Grand Lodge.

The Grand Lodge has been opened according to the usual formes, and it has been proceeded to the election of the Officers for the ensuing year, and the Brethren whose name follow have been duly elected :

THE BRETHREN :

M. Léfebvre, Merchant, *R.·. W.·. Grand-Master,*

J. B. Desbois, Counsellor at Law, *R.·. W.·. Deputy Grand-Master,*

Yves Le Monier, physician, *R.·. W.·. Senior Grand Warden,*

Augustin Macarty, Mayor, *R.·. W.·. Junior Grand Warden,*

N. Visinier, Master of Languages, *R.·. W.·. Grand Secretary,*

John Baptiste Pinta, Gold-Smith, *R.·. W.·. Grand Treasurer,*

D. R. D. Desessart, Secretary of the Mayoralty *R.·. W.·. Grand Orator,*

John Pinard, Merchant, *R.·. W.·. Grand Tyler,*

Stephen Berthel, Merchant, *R.·. W.·. Grand Poursuivant,*

G. Debuys, Merchant, *R.·. W.·. Grand Marshal.*

151

Page two also contains interesting information, but again it isn't very clear. In the second paragraph, we learn of the election of officers for the ensuing year. Reading this paragraph and following the first page of the December 26th communication confirm that this was when the election took place. Regardless of confusion on when the election occurred, the new officers' list provides interesting information.

One of the most common phrases I've heard in Masonry when asked why something is being done is, "Because it has always been done that way." Well, not always. The titles associated with Grand Lodge officers are an example. Today, the Grand Master of the Grand Lodge of Louisiana is titled "Most Worshipful Grand Master." Before 1850, however, the office of the Grand Master was known as "Right Worshipful Grand Master." It's possible that this was the result of four of the five lodges that created the Grand Lodge of Louisiana holding their charters from the Grand Lodge of Pennsylvania. In Pennsylvania, the Grand Master is known as the Right Worshipful Grand Master.

By the 1830s, the title had changed a bit. The *office* of Grand Master was known as the Right Worshipful Grand Master, but when speaking of the Grand Master himself, it became known as "Most Worshipful Brother" and then his name. This change may have been from exposure to Grand Lodges that use the "Most Worshipful" manner of address. But in addition to how the Grand Master was addressed, other differences are shown.

Today, the Grand Wardens of the Grand Lodge of Louisiana are the Grand Junior Warden and Grand Senior Warden. Until 1850, however, they were the Junior Grand

Warden and Senior Grand Warden. The same is true for the Grand Deacons. In addition, only the *elected* Grand Officers are known today as Right Worshipful. This does not apply to the Grand Master and any Past Grand Masters who might be serving as Grand Secretary or Grand Treasurer. They are addressed as "Most Worshipful." But, prior to 1850, all appointed Grand Lodge Officers were Right Worshipful. This changed, like so many other things, after 1850. Exactly why it changed is not clear.

What I also find interesting is that following the name of each Mason (elected or appointed) is his occupation. This is not done today, and I am not sure why it was originally done. But it does clarify a rather important point. In later years, some Masonic history books have attempted to downplay the qualifications of the early Officers of the Grand Lodge of Louisiana. Suggestions have been made that they were unskilled, naive, unsophisticated, and not exactly high-quality individuals. A quick look at the Grand Lodge Officers shows that in addition to merchants, we find attorneys, physicians, and even the mayor of New Orleans. The 1818 Grand Master was one of the authors of the Louisiana Civil Code that is still in use today. These were *not* intellectually deficient individuals. It is very clear that they would have been highly respected wherever they chose to live.

[3]

The Lodge has then been shut until the General Grand Communication on the 10th. day of the 11th. Month of Masonry 5818.

At a Grand General Communication held in ample forme in the City of New-Orleans, on the 10th. day of the 11th. Month of Masonry of the year 5818, the R∴ W∴ Grand Officers elect, were severally installed according to the ancient usages into their respective offices, and being duly proclaimed they received the cordial and accustomed salutations of the brethren present.

The R∴ W∴ Grand Master, and the R∴ W∴ Senior Grand Warden, appointed immediately after, the Brethren Henry Mathieu and Peter Lartigue Mongrue, Senior and Junior Grand Deacons ;

And the Brother R∴ W∴ Grand Secretary has appointed the Brother Peter Morel de Guiramand, Deputy Grand Secretary.

It as been afterwards proceeded to the formation of the committees of the said Grand Lodge and the following brethren have been nominated, to wit :

Committee of Charity.	Committee of Account.
The B∴ Moreau Lislet,	The B∴ Macarty,
Macarty,	J. B. Desbois,
Le Monier,	Le Monier.
Le Noir.	

Committee of Correspon.	Committee of Information.
Moreau Lislet,	Debuys,
J. B. Desbois,	Chatry,
D. R. D. Desessart.	Pinard.

Now we see page three of the Proceedings. The first two paragraphs create a confusing situation. They suggest that the Grand Lodge Officers' installation was held in November of 1818, with the first two pages of the proceedings suggesting that the election was on December 26th. It's just not possible that the installation would be held a month before the election. It seems more likely that the election was held on November 10th, with the installation on December 26th.

What is also interesting is the appointment of the Grand Deacons. Appointments today are generally made by the Grand Master. The third paragraph states that the "RW Grand Master" and "RW Senior Grand Warden" appointed the Senior and Junior Grand Deacons.

Then in the fourth paragraph, it states that the RW Grand Secretary" appointed a "Deputy Grand Secretary."

The fifth paragraph begins with the nominations for various committees.

I find it interesting that rather than simply saying that the Grand Master appointed the committees, note is made that the ones appointed were nominated by the Grand Lodge. Of course, it could be that it was assumed that the Grand Master was speaking for the Grand Lodge. It is not clear.

[4]

Committee of Stewardship.

Congourdan,
Auguste Douce,
Chatry.

The Grand Lodge has then been shut in good harmony.

ACTIVE MEMBERS OF THE GRAND LODGE.

L. Moreau Lislet, *Counsellor at Law, Founder, Ex-Grand-Master,*

J. Soulié, *Past Grand-Master, Merchant, Founder,*

F. Dubourg, *Past Grand-Master Mercht. Founder,*

J. B. Labatut, *Merchant, Founder,*

Paul Lanusse, *Merchant, Founder,*

Thomas Urquhart, *Merchant, Founder,*

Joseph Tricou, *Merchant, Founder,*

P. Hardy, *Teacher, Founder,*

Charles Roche, *Book-Seller, Founder,*

Victor-Amédée Bonjean, *Goldsmith, Founder,*

Peter Delino, *Planter, Founder,*

Joseph Eyssalem, *Merchant, Founder,*

A. Guibert, *Cashier of the B. Bank of the State,*

William S. Hubert, *Merchant,*

Auguste Douce, *Cabinet-Maker,*

Spire Loquet, *Master of Languages,*

John Guadiz, *Dentiste,*

Caliste Congourdan, *Undertaker,*

Andrews Clavié, *Merchant,*

Page four of the Proceedings continues with appointed committees but then goes into a list of the Active Members of the Grand Lodge. This list is important as it highlights what would become a disappointing Masonic political decision made by the Grand Lodge in 1850.

Today, the Active Members of the Grand Lodge of Louisiana are the three principal officers of each lodge, the Grand Lodge Officers, and the Past Grand Masters. But prior to 1850, Past Masters of all constituent lodges were also Active Members of the Grand Lodge with voting rights.

The turmoil of the mid-1800s has been covered in other papers and may be covered again in later papers. But, for now, it is sufficient to say that the decision to remove Past Masters from Active Membership was a move to assure that the new 1850 element in the Grand Lodge was not outvoted. It seems that it was a purely political decision. Regardless, before 1850, Past Masters were considered an active part of the Grand Lodge.

Now, one more interesting thing about this page. You will notice about two-thirds down the page is what seems to be a smudging out of a name. In many old documents, we find smudges and letters covered by discolored paper or flecks of paper covering words. In this case, however, the smudges seem to have been deliberate, and someone's name seems to have been covered up. We'll come back to this name removal on the last page.

[5]

Joseph Le Noir, *Hatter,*
J. B. Gilly, *Merchant,*
L. M. Renaud, *Merchant,*
G. W. Morgan, *Shérif,*
N. Mioton, *Confectioner,*
J. L. F. Chatry, *Clerck to a Notary,*
B. Bacas, *Cabinet-Maker,*
James Rouly, *Artist.*

Representatives of the Lodges of the Jurisdiction.

Gaspard Debuis W∴ Master,
L. M. Reynaud S∴ Warden, } *La Parfaite Union,*
J. B. Plauché J∴ Warden, *No.* 1.

No.
No. } Not represented, } *La Charité,*
No. *No.* 2.

Auguste Douce W∴ Master,
Manuel Fleytas S∴ Warden, } *La Concorde,*
H. Doiron J∴ Warden, *No.* 3.

J. Le Noir W∴ Master,
J. L. F. Chatry S∴ Warden, } *La Persévérance,*
F. Dissart J∴ Warden, *No.* 4.

J. B. Gilly W∴ Master,
B. Bacas S∴ Warden, } *l'Etoile Polaire,*
B. Grima J∴ Warden, *No.* 5.

No.
No. } Not represented, } *La Loge Friendship,*
No. *No.* 6.

J. Pinard, Representative
of the three Lodges } at the Stranger } *l'Union Fraternelle de la Charité, No.* 7, *Les Amis Réunis,* *No.* 8, *La Réunion à la Vertu,* *No.* 9.

Page 5 of the Proceedings closes the list of the Active Members of the Grand Lodge. The page goes on to provide the lodges represented at the Grand Lodge Communications. You will notice that Charity Lodge No. 2 is not represented. Charity Lodge would cease to exist just a few years after these Proceedings, about 1821.

Another lodge not represented was Friendship Lodge No. 6. Friendship lodge was organized in 1813 in Mobile, Alabama, and ceased to exist around the same time as Charity. Also, lodges l'Union Fraternelle de la Charité No. 7, Les Amis Réunis No. 8, and La Reunion a la Vertu No. 9 would not survive long.

L'Union Fraternelle de la Charité No. 7 was chartered by the Grand Lodge of Louisiana in Havana, Cuba, in 1815 and turned in its charter in 1820. Les Amis Réunis No. 8 was chartered by the GL in Vera Cruz, Mexico, in 1816. The lodge ceased to exist soon after this GL Communication was held. La Reunion a la Vertu No. 9 was chartered by the Grand Lodge in Campeche, Mexico, on the Yucatan Peninsula in 1817. It ceased to exist about 1821.

The Louisiana lodge created in Mobile is very interesting, but I also find the lodges created in Cuba and Mexico most interesting as well. Louisiana had a very close relationship with Freemasonry in both Cuba and Mexico for many years.

[6]

J. P. Morel de Guiramand, Representative . . . . }	*l'Etoile Flamboyante,* No. 10.
J. Pinard, Representative }	*Le Temple de la Divine Pastorale,* No. 11.
J. P. Morel de Guiramand, Representative . . }	*La Vérité,* No. 12.
Gaspard Debuys, Representative . . . }	*l'Union,* No. 13.
J. Pinard, Representative }	*La Rectitude,* No. 14.

Expulsions.

Anthony Herès, *No.* 3. *New-Orleans.*
Lewis Romano, *No.* 3. *New-Orleans.*
James Chauvin, *No.* 4. *New-Orleans.*

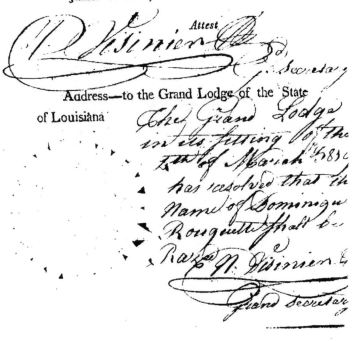

Attest

Address—to the Grand Lodge of the State of Louisiana

Page 6 of the Proceedings continues the list of lodges with l' Etoile Flamboyante No. 10 chartered in 1817 in Baton Rouge, LA, Le Temple de la Divine Pastorale No. 11 in 1818 in Matanzas, Cuba, Le Vérité No. 12 in 1818 in Donaldsonville, LA; L'Union No. 13 in 1818 in Natchitoches, LA, and La Rectitude No. 14 in 1818 in Havana, Cuba.

It looks to be a busy time for the Grand Lodge chartering lodges, especially outside its jurisdiction. More lodges were chartered in Cuba, Mexico, and Alabama in the next few years. Unfortunately, none of these lodges lasted very long.

The page ends with the printed names of those expelled from the Grand Lodge.

The proceedings are then attested to with the signature of the Grand Secretary, but it is not yet quite finished. A handwritten note at the bottom of the page is very interesting. The note is signed by the Grand Secretary.

If you remember, on page four, there was what looked like a name smudged out towards the bottom of the page. Well, it turns out that there was a name smudged out. The handwriting is difficult to read, but a close examination provides the following information, "The Grand Lodge in its sitting of the 9th of March 58 ... and it's not legible, maybe 16 as in 1816, but I'm not sure. I can't make out the final part of the date. But it goes on to say, "has resolved that the name of Dominique ROUGUETTE (maybe) shall be razen. (Razen is an antiquated word meaning erased.)

Clearly, this individual did something to cause his expulsion or, at the least, removal from the list of Active Members of the Grand Lodge. I can find no similar name in any of the existing later Grand Lodge Proceedings, and the earlier ones don't exist. Unless more information is discovered, whoever he was and whatever he did, his name is gone.

The two Proceedings examined in this paper cover only ten pages of information. But there is no doubt that we are far richer for having these ten small pages. Those who believe innovations do not and cannot occur in Freemasonry are simply in error. There is no debate on this matter. Masonic bodies have changed their practices and nature, sometimes quite dramatically, over the years. We change at the will of the members or at the will of small groups who are in power.

Those who reach any level of leadership in Masonry must realize that their role is to serve and not control. For those who fail to do so or when small groups have managed to take control of Masonic bodies, confusion in the Temple will result. Masonic philosophy teaches us that we are all on the level. We all have jobs to do in the Temple of Masonry. Leadership is a job that those with leadership skills must perform. Being a Masonic leader does not mean that we are better, smarter, or more important than other Masons. It only means that we have a different job which we must perform to the best of our ability. We all work for the betterment of ourselves and Freemasonry as a whole. We do not hold jobs in Masonry to feed our ego or gain power.

Change is inevitable in all of Masonry. But we must be on guard against change forced for the betterment of a few at the cost of the many. Change that is in harmony with the teachings of Freemasonry results in growth and prosperity. Change that ignores the whole or is the result of a desire to build up the whole to maintain the desires of a few will result in ultimate failure.

We are not Operative Freemasons who perform harsh physical labor to earn our pay. Our pay is self-improvement, and our work is learning, understanding, and living the teachings of Freemasonry. We should learn and then teach. Our Masonic lodges and bodies must follow the philosophy of Freemasonry or they become no more than vanity clubs. We are one with our teachings, or we are not. The choice is ours. I hope you follow the path of Light.

Peace.

About The Author

Michael R. Poll (1954 - present) is the owner of Cornerstone Book Publishers and editor of the *Journal of The Masonic Society*. He is a Fellow and Past President of The Masonic Society, a Fellow of the Philalethes Society, a Fellow of the Maine Lodge of Research, Member of the Society of Blue Friars, and Full Member of the Texas Lodge of Research.

A New York Times Bestselling writer and publisher, he is a prolific writer, editor, and publisher of Masonic and esoteric books. He is also the host of the YouTube channel "New Orleans Scottish Rite College."

As time permits, he travels and speaks on the history of Freemasonry, with a particular focus on the early history of the Scottish Rite.

He was born in New Orleans, LA and lives a peaceful life with his wife and two sons.

Thank you for buying this Cornerstone book!

For over 25 years now, we've tried to provide the Masonic community with quality books on Masonic education, philosophy, and general interest. Your support means everything to us and keeps us afloat. Cornerstone is by no means a large company. We are a small family owned operation that depends on your support.

Please visit our website and have a look at the many books we offer as well as the different categories of books.

If your lodge, Grand Lodge, research lodge, book club, or other body would like to have quality Cornerstone books to sell or distribute, write us. We can give you outstanding books, prices, and service.

Thanks again!

Cornerstone Book Publishers
1cornerstonebooks@gmail.com
http://cornerstonepublishers.com

Living Freemasonry
A Better Path to Travel
by Michael R. Poll
6×9 Softcover 180 pages
ISBN: 9781934935958

The Particular Nature of Freemasons
by Michael R. Poll
6x9 Softcover 156 pages
ISBN 9781613423462

The Scottish Rite Papers
A Study of the Troubled History of the Louisiana and
US Scottish Rite in the Early to Mid-1800s
by Michael R. Poll
6x9 Softcover 240 pages
ISBN 9781613423448

Measured Expectations
The Challenges of Today's Freemasonry
by Michael R. Poll
6×9 Softcover 180 pages
ISBN: 9781613422946

A Lodge at Labor
Freemasons and Masonry Today
by Michael R. Poll
6x9 Softcover 180 pages
ISBN 1613421834

Cornerstone Book Publishers
www.cornerstonepublishers.com

A Masonic Evolution
The New World of Freemasonry
by Michael R. Poll
6x9 Softcover 176 pages
ISBN 9781613423158

10,000 Famous Freemasons
4 Vol. Softcover Edition
by William Denslow
Foreword by Harry S. Truman
Cornerstone Foreword by Michael R. Poll
8.5 x 11, Softcover 2 Volumes 1,515 pages
ISBN 1887560319

Seeking Light
The Esoteric Heart of Freemasonry
by Michael R. Poll
6×9 Softcover 156 pages
ISBN: 1613422571

An Encyclopedia of Freemasonry
by Albert Mackey
Revised by William J. Hughan and Edward L. Hawkins
Foreword by Michael R. Poll
8.5 x 11, Softcover 2 Volumes 960 pages
ISBN 1613422520

Robert's Rules of Order: Masonic Edition
Revised by Michael R. Poll
6×9 Softcover 212 pages
ISBN: 1613422318

Cornerstone Book Publishers
www.cornerstonepublishers.com

Made in the USA
Middletown, DE
21 October 2023

41205768R00109